Moments at Mid Century:
a memoir

*MIT students and their communist professor

*Sputnik stuns the White House

*The Genius at Polaroid

Robert M. Briber

Moments at Mid Century:
a memoir

Robert M. Briber

Foreword

I write about people and events I knew over a dozen years in the mid 20ᵗʰ Century. I was young and had a lot to learn; this little book is about some of those things. There's not much about what I felt or thought; I was more interested in what I did and where I was going.

These memorable years included time spent as a MIT student and tell stories about some of my friends, time spent as student body president faced with student support for a communist professor and other issues, and time spent as a White House staffer when it dealt with "Sputnik."

Finally, I describe my time as a research administrator at Polaroid as Edwin Land's Polaroid Corporation introduced its widely anticipated color film. I do not include much about the years spent after I left Polaroid.

Two or three times, in the section, "On Crossing Harvard Bridge," my account has been created from descriptions given me by others. I wasn't there for the slide rule incident, for example, nor with the fraternity president as he talked with a failing student. This seemed OK at the time because I was confident the incidents occurred, if somewhat exaggerated. My accounts later, from the time I won the fateful election to my final days at Polaroid, are as accurate as I can make them.

I started this book after I graduated from MIT with a Master's degree and twenty-two months as Lieutenant in the US Army Chemical Corps during the Korean conflict. It lay uncompleted for years and for a time I thought I had lost it. I added to it later with notes from my time at Polaroid and finished it in my retirement.

Several people gave me important support both during the years in question and subsequently in writing about them:

My lovely wife Sylvia, whose influence colors every page, has to be recognized first. She was unwavering, faithful and believing throughout a long process. Her nephew's spouse, Heather Ciociola, proofread my text carefully and usefully. Lidia Pasamanick, dear friend and neighbor, gave me useful advice. In his continuing support, my son, Rob, discovered to my surprise that two patents were issued in my name after I left Polaroid. He also stepped in several times to extricate me from various computer problems.

I have to recognize friends at MIT, Julie and Fred Fassett, who were such an influence and saw me through important, formative years, and others, students like my fraternity brothers and dorm resident Dana Ferguson, who did much of the real work to get me elected student body president. I'm very grateful to Jim Killian, a great public servant, who made it all possible.

Meroe Morse, Edwin Land's principal assistant and my original boss at Polaroid, was very influential to my story. Sadly, she passed on a few years after I left the Company.

I owe each of these people and others a great deal. Thank you.

And to repeat myself, thanks, Sylvie.

Contents

1948
On Crossing Harvard Bridge

The Life I Leave · 3
MIT: A New World · 5
The Best View · 7
My First Friend · 10
Big Decision · 13
Boy on a Bunk · 15
Class Begins · 18
Beacon Street · 21
Argument · 23
Everyone Has a Story · 26
First Snow · 36
"Do You Love Me?" · 40
We End a Term · 46
Hell Week · 50
The Election · 55

1952
A Gun, a Panty Raid and a Communist

Student Body President · 59
"I Am Afraid for My Life" · 61
The Dean Incites a Riot · 63
MIT... a Communist Front? · 67
My First Briefcase · 76

1958
A Year at the White House

Our Digs · 83
Meetings, Travels and Disappointments · · · · · · · · · · · · · · · · · · 86
Radar Contact With Venus · 89

1957
Polaroid: Behind Blue Doors

Back to Cambridge · 95
My Story · 97
The Company · 100
The Man · 102
His Space · 105
The People · 109
The Research · 122
The Mood · 128
Diversification as a Laboratory Project · · · · · · · · · · · · · · · · · · 134
My Work · 136
A Harem? · 140
Conversations · 142
Power Struggle · 145
Stockholders See the Film · 149
Document Copy · 151
I Quit · 155
From a Distance · 157

2013
Epilogue

This Life Goes On · 163

On Crossing Harvard Bridge
1948

The Life I Leave

I left Denver and another life two days ago.

Mother and Dad stood in the train station and waved and I waved back. I was leaving. Mother tried hard not to show she was crying. I didn't cry, at least not really, but I did go into the washroom as soon as they were out of sight to wash my fingernails.

Certain values were part of the life I was leaving. Men, even fathers, couldn't cry but they could remind a son about values. I didn't need to be reminded that this particular value, cleanliness, extended even to fingernails.

The permanence and sanctity of marriage was another value. In an epochal event of my childhood a cousin divorced her husband for philandering. From that day on we spoke of her only in embarrassed, hushed tones. No telling how my cousin's ill-fated marriage began; we didn't want to know, much less discuss it with others. In our world at the time one didn't even kiss until the third date.

My cousin took her two small children and moved to Australia.

Doing constructive work was yet another value. My father was born in Pennsylvania in 1890, fourteen years after his beloved Colorado became a state. He spent his adult life in and around mining. A college graduate, Republican and a kind and gentlemanly man, he treated patriotism and the economy as different faces of the same coin. I think he felt he was building his adopted state job by job. To do so was his ultimate patriotism.

3

It was my good fortune to travel with him occasionally. One day, while waiting for him to finish his work at a mill processing ore for its metals, I tried to fish in the stream that cascaded the tailings down the columbine-dotted hill to a larger stream below. I had a stick, a safety pin and a string, hardly sophisticated fishing gear.

"Look at that, Dad," I said when he came out, as if I could catch a fish with the gear I had. "I can't fish here. The water's gray with all that junk."

"I know, Bob," he said, almost apologetically, "but those are jobs. Those are jobs."

MIT: A New World

Today was a very important day. I walked across Harvard Bridge toward my chosen college, the Massachusetts Institute of Technology.

Later I would hear it said that the water beneath me was so dirty that it was too thick to pour and too thin to shovel. Today I didn't see the water nor did I feel the insistent wind that tugged at me and blew up noisy whitecaps. Later I would hear it said that MIT, the "Institute," was a factory and differed from other factories only in that its product was human. Right now the only things I knew were the things I saw, and right now my eyes were wide with wonder. Excitement pushed everything else out of my mind. Today was a very important day.

Abruptly I realized that someone walked across the bridge toward me, returning from the Cambridge side of the river.

"Hello," I said.

The passerby looked at me with surprise. "Hi," he returned, and walked on.

"Nice looking guy," I thought. "He knows his way around. I'll bet he's at least a junior."

When I reached the Institute I could hardly control my excitement. I ran up the long stairs of the main, grand building, stopped and looked with awe at its great gray pillars and broad windows and into its grand lobby. This was the iconic image of MIT: a gray-stone and domed great building in Cambridge facing the Charles River and Boston.

The door in front of me opened automatically, propelled by an electric eye. This was magic for a boy from another world. I walked through and watched others walk through. I stood in the lobby and read the great inscriptions many feet above me. I struck off down a hallway and wandered this way and that, touching, feeling, smelling, seeing, and living in sensations. I lost myself in dim corridors and found myself in bright entrances. "Cavitation Pit" said one door; "Radioactivity Laboratory" said another. I read them all with delight and mystified eyes. They were marvelous names.

I stopped in front of a campus map. Purpose returned to my wandering when I read the title "Chemical Engineering." I wanted to be a chemical engineer, whatever that was. I liked high school chemistry, especially the teacher, and I had read somewhere a paragraph about chemical engineers.

Here was their building, worth all the admiration I could give it. In the center was a large laboratory filled with red and black and clear glass pipes two stories high. A grimy figure in a T-shirt worked at something with a wrench. I watched him out of the corner of my eye; I shouldn't distract him by watching too closely. I watched and walked on.

When the bite of hunger called me to awareness of the time I realized I had walked for hours. I couldn't spend any more time this way; the days ahead were filled with things to do. Fraternity Rush Week started tomorrow. Where was I to live? In a week or so classes began. So much to learn and do.

The sun was just setting as I worked my way out and back across the Harvard Bridge. I stopped halfway across to look back at my college and my new life. The sun cast a shadow from the west across the courtyard in front of the building. Its grand dome stood out in the last sunlight.

The Best View

The best view of MIT is offered by walking across that bridge we considered misnamed, the "Harvard Bridge."

The MIT academic buildings were built with the solidity and pride that befitted an old New England school. The grand academic building to the right is quiet gray stone, shaped in the form of a gigantic, sharp-cornered "U." Its width is parallel to the river and stretches 365 paces from west to east, by actual count by a group of fraternity pledges. The arms of the "U" reach toward the river and enclose the largest body of ornamental grass on campus.

The arms of the "U" are topped with towers engraved with the names of famous scientists and are capped with the soft green that copper warrants when exposed to salt air and wind. The arms seem to reach toward the city of Boston across the river, as if they were not content with enclosing the grass but wanted to encompass that city as well. After all, MIT had started life years before carrying the nickname "Boston Tech."

The main building demonstrates all the stable strength an architect could provide. Broad steps radiate down from great glass and steel doors in the center of the building. Huge granite columns rise above the doors and carry a broad expanse of gray stone with the inscription, in letters two feet tall, "MASSACHVSETTS INSTITVTE OF TECHNOLOGY." Finally, above this tongue-twisting inscription and completing the rise of the building, is an enormous dome.

Perhaps the stateliness of this main entrance, the dome or the impression of dignity it conveys is a little too much for students. Most student publications at least once a year cartoon its grandeur. One attempt pictured the building with the dome removed and a caption accusing Harvard students of pilfering. Other attempts pictured the dome as part of an enormous ice cream sundae or as a college stadium or swimming pool turned upside down by the architect's mistake.

Or perhaps the student body is, beneath its cynical appearance, really quite proud of its great dome. The yearbook, one publication kept by a sentimental graduate, invariably accentuates all the dignity of the dome with two or three rich pictures.

MIT as seen from the Charles River

East of this main building is the library with stretches of glass and visible rows of books. A focus of student life, a student union called "Walker Memorial," is next and behind that stand three old dormitories of the same solid gray. Still farther east, less deep now for Cambridge factories edge closer to the river, is the President's house with its continuity of the ubiquitous gray mood.

Three dissimilar dormitories stretch along the river to the left for a visitor crossing the Harvard Bridge. The school bought an old hotel and converted it into a dormitory when older dormitories overflowed. Then they built a new dormitory when the hotel overflowed, and before that dormitory was finished they bought another hotel. This hopscotch process shows up in a lack of continuous architecture but nobody, much less the students, seems to mind. Behind this human and comfortable hodgepodge of buildings are the playing fields and a gymnasium.

West Campus on the left seems separated by Massachusetts Avenue and nearly by a philosophy from East Campus on the right — home and play on the left, work and study on the right.

My First Friend

I walked back across the Harvard Bridge toward Boston, retracing the steps I had taken earlier. Ahead of me lay Beacon Hill with its gold topped State House glistening in the last rays of sunlight; here and there a building caught fire as its windows flashed in the setting sun. I saw white sailed dories for the first time and felt the exhilaration of skimming a light and fragile boat across choppy gray water. The trees lining the Esplanade, a long park along the Boston side of the river, were in shadow but still green and beautiful.

I crossed this bridge many times and it came to mean Boston to me. This, however, was the first time. My awe was heightened by the heraldry of a spectacular gray, green, and gold New England day gloriously displayed by a setting sun.

I turned to the right on Beacon Street without hesitation for my parents and I had studied maps and found the best place to stay. Several fraternities invited me to spend Rush Week with them but that didn't seem like a good idea. The Hotel Fensgate, however, was on Beacon Street at the end of a row of fraternity houses. Buzz Urling, another Denver freshman, and I planned to stay together for Rush Week, so I had written the Fensgate to learn they had a triple room if we would share it with a third freshman. So far so good.

I met the third student, Jack Lewis, earlier. He was the first classmate I was to meet in this new world. Perhaps five feet ten inches tall, he had dark hair and a pleasant, if diffident, personality. Friends and acquaintances yet to be described piled up after that.

Many friends proved more engaging, but Jack Lewis was the first. His unfamiliarity with MIT surprised me with how much about life here I already knew. Lewis wanted to be a mechanical engineer. His father ran a machinery company in Ohio and he planned to join him. He put a picture of a girl on his desk, a picture so big it crowded the desk. To write her he had to move the picture.

I returned from my explorations to find Lewis in our room. "Hi, Jack," I said, "Where's Buzz?"

"He's gone to the ball game with some Beta Theta Pi's. The Red Sox are playing the Yankees."

"He's gone out?" I was surprised. "Was he going to have dinner with them? I didn't think rushing began until tomorrow."

"All he said was not to wait up for him. Why would I wait up for him?" Lewis paused from the letter he had started. "It must have been all right. Nobody said anything about it. They seemed like a nice bunch of guys. I've got a date with them tomorrow. Are you supposed to call them Beta Theta Pi's or just Betas?"

"Betas, I think. My brother was a . . Beta Theta Pi at the Colorado School of Mines. He always called them Betas. He wrote a letter about me to this chapter."

"Hunh. I never thought of that. Does it help to have people write letters for you?"

"I think so. My older brother was a Sigma Chi here, and they asked me to dinner tomorrow night."

"You had a brother here? When was that?" Lewis was surprised.

"He graduated in 1943. He studied metallurgy."

"Are you going to study metallurgy?"

"No, I don't think so . . . Dad said that there were enough things to do without his sons competing with each other. He knew a couple of brothers in Denver who had a sporting goods store and one day got into an argument about a five dollar bill, and nobody, not even their kids, could talk to each other after that. They split up. Each of them has his own sporting goods store now."

"Are you going to join Sigma Chi?" he asked. Lewis paused a minute, but then went on without seeming to expect an answer. "I hope I'm bid to join a fraternity."

"My brother, the one who came here to Tech, says that anyone who wants to join bad enough can. He figures that a lot of fraternities are not worth joining. He said a lot of guys would be better off living in a dormitory."

Not a word escaped Lewis. He seemed relieved both at the thought that almost anyone could join a fraternity and that someone said some fraternities were not worth joining. On his face was an earnest, honest want: he wanted to join a fraternity.

Lewis and I talked for a long time when we met earlier. He talked about the girl whose picture crowded his desk and their future. They were going to marry in two years and she would come live with him in Boston. He missed his parents, too, but his father was visiting him in two days to see how Rush Week was going.

I listened to him with quiet interest. The part about marrying in two years was a new idea. Marriage was still something for the future, something way off and hazy. Lewis took it as so much a matter of course that I decided to think it out at length. . . .Sometime.

Later that night I lay in bed waiting for sleep to come. Dreams and plans whirled around in my mind. Today I had come to Boston. Today I saw the Massachusetts Institute of Technology. Tomorrow it all began in earnest.

Big Decision

Lewis and I met again the next morning and the next evening and again the following morning, but we were either too rushed or too tired to talk. Rush Week was in full swing.

Late the second afternoon I came into the room hurriedly to wash up for a dinner invitation. Lewis' father was in the room, and the boy talked hard and with concentration about the fraternities he had visited. I stayed long enough to hear the complete story on one fraternity and the start of a second.

The father listened but Lewis wasn't just talking, he was asking. He didn't know it, and perhaps his father didn't know it either, but he was asking. This was his first big college decision, and he was away from home, "What am I supposed to do?"

"Bob," Lewis asked, after his father had left for the night, "do you really think the Betas are all right? It's good to join a big nationwide fraternity, but it's not the national fraternity a guy lives with. He lives with the guys right at his own school."

"Sure they're all right. They're a good bunch." He could ask all he wanted but I was not going to tell him what to do.

Lewis seemed to hesitate and then, as I started to leave the room, "I wish you'd join the Betas so then I would, too."

"OK, Jack." I said. "But I've gotta decide pretty soon, maybe even tonight."

I rang the doorbell at the Sigma Chi house at seven fifteen the next morning. The rush chairman was in his pajamas but could still muster sufficient dignity to pin the pledge button on my jacket with a bit of ceremony. I said thank you and after shaking hands all around with the few early risers, I walked to the other two fraternities I had been invited to join and told them my decision. Now I had earned the right to join Sigma Chi.

"Hey, what's that?" Jack asked after I returned to our room, hurrying over to look at the small blue shield with its tiny white cross in my lapel.

"It's a pledge button."

"Whose?"

"Sigma Chi."

"Gee whiz. Sigma Chi. Hunh. They must be a pretty good fraternity."

"I think they're the best." I believed it but my voice carried more conviction than I meant it to carry. I was pleased with the decision but not overwhelmed.

"You know, I never went to see them." Lewis' was almost querulous. "I had a date with them yesterday but the Theta Xi's had me break it so I could see them again."

"What the hell," I said, seeing a way out of an awkward conversation. "Here a guy makes a big decision like a fraternity and his buddy doesn't even congratulate him or anything."

"Oh, yeah, congratulations. Congratulations all to hell."

I packed my clothes, the gray slacks, white shirt and maroon cord jacket that were to become almost my school uniform and prepared to move out. We talked of clothes and the hotel bill and how I had accepted the bid ("I just walked in and said I would like to join.") and how we'd meet in class. From that day on, without conscious desire that it should be so, Lewis and I drew apart, finally to become merely nodding acquaintances.

Boy on a Bunk

While Lewis and I dealt with Rush Week, and on the same morning that marked the end of our real camaraderie, the Associate Dean of Students, Fred Fassett, happened on another freshman. The boy was another candidate for fraternity membership but was housed in a dormitory for those who couldn't afford or couldn't arrange a hotel room.

MIT furnished bunks, dressers and desks in the only slightly converted army barracks that served as freshman dormitories at the time. The rooms were large and musty and impersonal. The beds were covered with army blankets and the desks were scarred and scratched. Twelve men lived in each room; the property of each was distinguished from the next by an imaginary line drawn by separating beds a foot more than necessary. It was an unpleasant environment overall, especially for a homesick freshman.

The Dean passed each room and gave it a hurried glance. He knew and deplored the effect the rooms had on freshman; part of his purpose in making the tour was to try to liven the atmosphere. Hurrying down the second floor hall, a movement in the corner bunk of one of the large rooms caught his eye. The boy sat there.

He was staring at the floor when the Dean came in to adjust one of the beds and startled, picked up a magazine and pretended to be engrossed in an advertisement. The Dean emptied an astray on the desk near the boy. He turned to open a window. The day showed promise of being hot and muggy. He began straightening the bed next to the one where the boy sat slowly rifling pages.

"You know," he said more to the bed than to the boy, "Being in the Army during the war sure taught me one thing. I can't bear to see a wrinkled bunk." The boy looked up and the Dean, as if pleased at the glance, winked. "I was a Captain. My men were afraid of me." He finished the bed and immediately sat down on it.

"Are you new around here? I don't remember seeing you before."

The boy started to speak, choked, and nodded.

"Well, then, it's about time you and I got to know each other. I'm Fred Fassett, and I work in the Dean's Office." He smiled a slow, engaging smile and spoke gently. "When I was in the Army, everybody was afraid of me. Now I can't even get a rise out of students. They just laugh at me." When the boy returned his smile, Fassett seemed delighted but stayed the same stodgy, conservative Associate Dean of Students.

"You know," he continued, "I'll bet you came early for Rush Week. Where's your home?"

"Roswell, New Mexico, sir."

"You live in Roswell? No fooling. I've been near there. Did you ever think of going to the Military School?"

"Yes, sir, . . but. . . well, I want to study mathematics and they don't have much."

"I think you made a wise choice," said the Dean. "I think the Army is a good vocation for some people, and I think that military training is good for a lot of people, but for you and me, we'll take civilian life, eh?"

The boy and the Dean talked for ten minutes. At first, slowly, the talk was in question and answer form. Gradually the boy talked more and the gently clowning tactics of the Dean ceased. They talked of many things: the weather, New England, MIT, mathematics. Just a moment before the Dean left they talked of the thing uppermost in their minds.

"You know, sir," the boy was almost loquacious now, "my sister likes fraternity men and she wanted me to come back for Rush Week." The boy shook his head but the sadness in his eyes said more than his words. "But I don't know. I don't know if I'd do very well in a fraternity."

"John, you're wise to think about it that way. There are a lot of men hereabouts who don't give a damn about fraternities. Why, did you know that for every man that comes back for Rush Week, two stay away? They don't even bother to come."

"I thought everybody came to Rush Week."

"No, they don't. More stay away than come, and maybe it's just as well. Fraternity life doesn't suit everybody. When I was in college I didn't join one and I'm not sorry. You go around to some of the fraternities and look and if you don't like what you see, you just come back here. Once school starts you'll find a bunch of fine guys living here."

As he left, the Dean elicited the boy's promise to come see him in a week or ten days. *"More went unsaid than said,"* Fassett thought to himself — and told me later — as he hurried off. *"Damn. Damn. Damn. Been here three days and already he thinks he's a failure."*

Class Begins

The forms had been filled out and the long lines waited through to completion. MIT greeted us with a short get-acquainted retreat. I had gleaned the essentials for a beginner, which building was which, which classrooms were mine. My wondering eyes only slowly returned to normal for every now and then I happened on corridors or even a building I hadn't seen before. Now I was starting school, in a newly acquired status as a Sigma Chi pledge.

Every pleasant morning most Sigma Chis crossed the Harvard Bridge on foot, a few hitchhiked and one or two drove their own cars. I didn't realize until the second morning that several hundred other students crossed the bridge every morning.

Jerry Laufs and I crossed on foot that first September morning, leaving twenty minutes early. There we went, two eager freshmen, both a little over six feet tall, walking together to new adventure. Twenty minutes early! How we'd laugh a few years later to think of our nervous enthusiasm.

We had homework to prepare before the first class. I didn't understand the assignment and hadn't done it. "Gee, Jerry," I said, "I hate to go to class without doing the homework. I want to get off to a good start, but this doesn't seem to be a very good way to do it. Did you do anything more on it after I went to bed?"

"I worked about an hour with Johnny Harris. He still has his freshman homework. He had the answers."

"You did?" That hurt. I had hoped, after talking about the problems, that Laufs wouldn't do the homework.

"Yeah. I was going to show it to you but you were in bed."Laufs enjoyed the walk. It was a crisp and clear autumn morning. The wind invigorated him.

"Hey, would you look at that!!" He pointed across the bridge to the other sidewalk. A girl in gray flannel slacks and a colorful sport shirt was striding to class. We watched her stride past several clusters of men. If she could prove feminine superiority by walking fast she succeeded.

"Hey, isn't she something? She's even got a slide rule," Laufs said.

We walked on for fifty feet lost in contemplation. The girl's hurried and purposeful walk showed determination. We watched her, bemused, and finally an explanation occurred to me. "I'll bet she did the damn homework."

I walked home at noon in better spirits. Two other freshmen Sigma Chis, Al Staples and Joe Miller, were in my section. Already we were friends.

Al Staples was a short, aggressive freshman, a military veteran. He had started school some years before but had dropped out into the Navy. He was quick to tell you he had crossed and recrossed the Atlantic but slow to admit he had never seen action. WWII veterans, like Staples, made up about half of our freshman class and, like others, the GI bill paid for his college education.

Joe Miller was a soft-spoken, soft-faced, brown haired recent high school graduate, like me. He had big, liquid brown eyes and a devastating, slightly cynical sense of humor.

"What was that guy's name?" I asked, about the math teacher.

"Middlescoff, or something like that," Staples answered.

"Isn't he an odd duck, though?" Miller said. "Did you notice that the bottom button on his shirt was gone; his belly button was waving around like a one-eyed sailor. 'Zis is ze way you solve ze first problem.'" Miller mimicked the professor to perfection.

"You know, that's a hell of an introduction. Our first big day, our first class. Calculus, a tough subject. We had homework. Twenty green freshmen sit around, tense and nervous. Boom, the door opens. A guy minces across the room, shirt open at the waist, 'Zis is ze way you solve ze first problem,' he says, and we're off."

I laughed at first but I stopped laughing. The professor had made peace with us before the class ended, introduced himself properly and excused those without homework. I was relieved and lost myself in the subject of the class. I had forgotten the first weird minutes.

"What'd you expect? This is a college, man, not a playground." Staples answered Miller's mimicry. "When I was here before, I knew Mathews — the physics guy — pretty well. He's all right. I'll bet I can do all right in that course."

"Who's Mathews? We were talking about Middlescoff," I asked.

"Didn't you see him put his name on the blackboard? He's the physics professor. I was in the section he taught before I left."

"How long were you here before you were drafted?" Miller asked.

"A term and about two weeks. I wasn't drafted. I enlisted. I left just after I got initiated."

"You've been initiated? That makes you an 'active,' doesn't it?" Miller went on. "Maybe you can tell me why do they call themselves 'actives'? The pledges knock themselves out every Saturday afternoon at work sessions. We go to pledge meetings every Wednesday and learn all sorts of stuff, and they call you guys actives."

Staples looked closely at Miller. The question annoyed him. Miller broke into his characteristic slow grin and Staples' irritation faded. "You'd better be careful who you ask questions like that," Staples said. "Pledges should know their place," was his message.

We walked on, quiet for several steps, before I mentioned calculus again. The subject of 'actives' was dropped.

Beacon Street

I had seen the back of historic Beacon Hill that first afternoon when I walked home from Cambridge. For a boy from a small western town it was invested with majesty. Beacon Hill was the home of the bankers and shippers who made the history of Boston and of so much of America. It was crowded now, and an uncontrolled fire could destroy it, but still it was magical and impressive.

Beacon Street, "upper" Beacon Street, starts on Beacon Hill. The Massachusetts State House tops the hill in grandeur. Upper Beacon Street houses line the street next to the State House. They had been, and some still were, the homes of families with names like Cabot or Lodge or Saltonstall.

Across from the Boston Common and the Boston Garden, upper Beacon Street still exhibited many of the traits that earned it fame. Many of these houses were stately and withdrawn, rumored to have the most exquisite interiors. Cadillacs and Packards parked in the street and now and again a properly dressed chauffeur would drive one away. Beacon Hill and Beacon Street clung to well-aged virtue like the prim and often elderly ladies who seemed to have inherited it.

Beacon Street continues on a straight westerly route through the area called Back Bay, with comfortable homes interspersed with rooming houses. Students from several different colleges live here and bring vigor to an old neighborhood.

Massachusetts Avenue, a few blocks farther west, crosses Beacon Street and connects Cambridge and Boston via the Harvard Bridge. Most of the services a student could want stand near this intersection: a Chinese laundry, a drug store, a bar and grill we called "The Espy" for "Esplanade," a tailor, and a church.

"Lower" Beacon Street (now), still straight but well-worn and a little tawdry, passes a monotonous collection of 1920s row houses stacked wall to wall in classic urban style. (Joe Miller, a stranger to that form of urban life, said that if one fell they'd all fall like a row of tin soldiers.) Some of the houses are in good repair; others, still served by direct current electricity, are sad and broken. One gained notoriety as a brothel but most are not even that distinctive. Several had been remodeled for fraternities, including the Sigma Chi fraternity house at number 532.

Beyond these houses, the Hotel Fensgate and across from it a huge dormitory for Boston University women, Charlesgate Hall, dominate the street. The neighborhood then ends with the "Fenway" and its small stream, the Fens. Beacon Street itself goes on but for us it ended at the Fens.

One day between Rush Week appointments, Lewis and I decided to explore a bit. Since upper Beacon Hill was far away to the East, we chose to walk along the "Fens," that lay just west of our Hotel. The Fens — strange name to a western boy, "Fens," — was a small and stagnant tributary to the Charles but still a green oasis in what was mostly a gray and sooty city.

From the banks of the Fens we could see our part of Boston with clear perspective. We learned, then and latter, that to the South lay Boston's grand museums; West was Fenway Park, home to the Boston Red Sox; North was the Charles River, Cambridge and its famous colleges. Our new home on Beacon Street, from its elegant beginnings to our fraternity row, promised to be part of a wonderful college town.

Argument

I shared a room on the fourth floor with my friend Joe Miller and two upperclassmen, but for an hour after dinner, a few weeks later, I was the only person in the room. I had come upstairs early to study. I could forego the coffee and conversation in the library that followed dinner, but I couldn't forego homework.

Gusts of wind pushed and tugged impatiently at the window and left pathways of white foam in the river below. The windows repulsed the wind but, undaunted, it went on its insistent way to play with bits of paper or perhaps women's hats, finally to find its way to Boston harbor. The wind was my constant companion as I studied.

Jerry Laufs came upstairs with me. His smaller two-person room adjoined my four-person room, and he also was alone. Once, in the hour that we studied alone, I asked him about a chemistry problem, but that was all the contact we had.

The door to my room burst open three times as each roommate announced his intention to study. After each came in there was hubbub and then gradually the quiet was broken less by careless noise and more by the careful rustle of papers and books, and of course the wind. Each student had his own preoccupation.

The second floor library of the Sigma Chi house, down two floors from our rooms, faced Beacon Street with several large windows. The walls were paneled with wood and the ceiling crisscrossed with stained oak supports.

Two easy chairs and two matching sofas covered in heavy brown leather and a large library table and window seats in deep red leather completed the room.

To validate the use of the term "library" three shelved walls contained dusty volume after dusty volume of abandoned books. Earlier in some year a pledge during his Hell Week duties had dusted off the backs of the books with a cloth he had just used to wash windows. The books, on close examination, were stained with the white residue that may work well on windows but not on book bindings.

The library was a room of pride. We entertained parents here. We greeted and engaged prospective pledges in conversation here. We used the room during the week for coffee after dinner, for meetings and bull sessions, occasionally even for study. On weekends it served as a convenient, quiet room with the darkness comfortable to amorous couples.

Had Jerry or I listened this evening instead of studying, we would have heard an argument in the library. Willie Peppler, junior, was speaking. "Yeah, of all the rotten deals. A bunch of chicken livered teetotalers say that a man can't even get a drink in the fraternity house. Here I left to fight the war and when I come back some jerks say I can't have a drink in the library — anywhere. Now the only thing a man can is do wait until Saturday night for a beer. A beer!"

After Willie left, the two continued the conversation. "You know, I think Willie's a good guy but I don't think there should be liquor in the fraternity house. God didn't intend people to drink. It's not right." said Howard Fast, freshman.

"Hogwash," said Tom Jennings, his classmate. He disagreed and was angered by the quick reference to God. "There's no harm in a man's drinking if he knows what he's doing."

"You guys want a cup of coffee? It's almost gone." George Dickson, an upperclassman, joined the group.

"Willy Peppler just told us about the liquor rules. We're talking about them," Fast said.

"Then I'll bet you heard the whole deal," Dickson smiled. "It's a rotten set-up, according to Willie. You see," Dickson explained, "what happened is that the Institute doesn't say 'yes' or 'no' to liquor, so every fraternity gets to decide its liquor rules for itself. Different fraternities have different rules."

"Alcohol's always been a big deal for us. We've decided we sort of don't want it, so we set up this system. If a man wants to drink he can as long as it's Saturday night and he stays downstairs and just drinks beer. He can come upstairs but he can't bring the beer up. Then when we have a big party we generally vote hard liquor into the house."

"Doesn't seem like a man would get much of a chance to learn how to drink," Jennings continued. "To me a guy's gotta learn sometime, and this is as good a time as any."

"Hell, he gets all the chance he needs. There's the Espy around the corner and the hotel next door," Dickson replied.

"If a guy wants a drink, he doesn't have to go far. Drinking during the week is not a good idea. Drinking and studying don't mix."

"I don't think it's good that it's so easy to get a drink. I don't think people should drink," said Fast.

The argument went on. Jennings wanted to drink in the house; he already was a heavy drinker. Fast disliked the practice, and fought against it vigorously with an occasional reference to God. Dickson forgot to be an elder statesman and joined in with vigor to defend the compromise.

The trio called ceasefire when the siren of a passing ambulance called their attention to the time. Each left to study begrudgingly.

Everyone Has a Story

Six weeks of college for a boy far away from home can be a hard and trying time. There he had been a successful high school senior in a familiar setting, and here an ordinary freshman far from home. Some take it and grow; others can't take it. A fraternity provides friends and acquaintances. Friends of any sort help, but the student and the things he brings with him smooth or roughen the weeks.

Tom Jennings, freshman pledge and the proponent of easier liquor rules, was handsome and knew it. He was not tall but straight and slight with cropped curly brown hair and features and complexion that could have been chiseled from marble. Quick with a quip and often in search of a cigarette, he could be clever and amusing but occasionally dogmatic and uncompromising. It was clear that he believed what he said about liquor.

He came back to the fraternity house at least one evening every weekend drunk, or nearly so. Nothing the house president nor Johnny Harris, his house-appointed big brother, did could stop him.

The fraternity president, Jim Veras, called Jennings into his room once before the early, six-week preliminary grades were posted. Veras was a serious student and a conscientious president. Maybe he could help if he could talk with Jennings; he wasn't doing well in his schooling and Veras knew it.

Veras' room was ideal for conferences; it was the only study room furnished with meetings in mind. Blond wood and leather-overstuffed chairs filled it and it was comfortable and close. Jennings and Veras could talk well there. Their conversation went something like this:

"Tom," Veras said when Jennings slouched into the room and sullenly sat down. "Tom, thanks for coming. I wanted a chance to talk with you. Johnny Harris, your mentor, wanted me to as well. He tells me you're having trouble with your studies. He wanted to know, and I want to know, if there is anything we can do to help."

"Thanks just the same, but no."

Veras watched while Jennings, barely settled into his chair, twisted a worn pack of cigarettes from his side pocket, straightened one and lit it. He blew the smoke out loudly. Veras pushed his chair into place and sat down. A moth fluttered out from behind the chair and flew at the one lighted lamp in the room.

"Look, Tom. You realize, don't you, that our purpose is to help you all we can? I'm not here to give you trouble. We feel responsible for your progress." Veras chose his words carefully. "I'll hate to write your parents that you're not getting along too well. I'd hate it a whole lot more if I have to say I don't think you're trying."

"No sense in your writing. I write," Jennings said quickly.

Veras responded, "I'm going to write parents. We do it for all freshmen. Why? Just so they know how their boy's getting along. Parents want to know." Veras smiled quietly and shifted his feet to the desk top.

"Well, don't worry about me. I'll be all right."

"I am going to write your parents." Veras feet came down with a thud. "I'm sure they'd like to know if you're having trouble."

"Sure they'd like to know. But Dad would just get mad, and Mother would be put out."

"Put out?"

"All right, so she'd be broken up. What do you want, a diagram?"

"Now take it easy, Tom. I'm doing it for your own good. Honest to God I'm just trying to help"

"Don't you worry about me."

"I am worrying." Veras paused. Jennings pulled at his cigarette until the end was ragged and wet. With disgust he ground it out and lit another.

"What does your father do?" Veras tried to release the tension.

"He runs a shipping line from Staten Island."

"Oh, I see! Is that why you are going to be a naval architect?"

"I guess so. I really don't give a damn."

Veras thought a minute. The boy was not lacking in intelligence; he was sharp enough in retorts and conversation to indicate plenty of capacity. *"But he says he doesn't give a damn."*

Veras relaxed and looked out his window. Through the black bars of a fire escape and the window's accumulated grime he watched a huge red neon "57" atop a Heinz factory across the river blink on and off, and on and off again.

The moth flitted and banged against the lamp. The light made a circle on the pale wood and the moth flew as if caught in a circular cage.

"He really acts like he doesn't care, but he's smart," Veras thought, *"I know he's smart. He's quick and he's impatient with slow thinkers. Probably he's impatient with me. But what's wrong?"*

"May I go now?" Jennings broke in impatiently. "I have to study."

"Don't run off for a minute. Look, Tom, don't you want to be a naval architect? You could go a long way with that degree."

"That's what they say. Swat that damn moth, would you? He's driving me nuts."

Veras got up, but the moth had disappeared. Standing, he turned: "Don't you believe that degree is worth something?"

"Oh, I don't know. I've known a lot of sharp guys who don't have a degree."

The work "sharp" stung Veras. "There's a lot more to life than just being sharp," he said.

"What?" Jennings' reply was hardly a question.

The moth appeared again and with furry thumps beat against the light.

Veras replied, "Well, there's professional ability, the ability to design and build the boats your father sails. There's a pride of accomplishment. There's money and recognition. And for a lot of us there's a deep down satisfaction that we're doing what we want to do and doing it well."

"Don't worry about me. I'll do what I want."

"Do you want to flunk out?"

"No."

"Well, then, you may flunk out if you keep on the way you're going." Jennings was quiet so Veras continued.

"Look, I've got to write your folks. Will you let me tell them you're really trying?"

"Tell them anything you like."

"I'm going to tell them the truth."

"All right, I'll try. I'll give it the old college try." Jennings paused for a moment and for the first time saw the anxiety in Veras' eyes and seemed to realize the President was truly trying to help. "All right, I'll try. I give you my word. . . may I leave now?"

"Sure. thanks for coming in."

Veras watched him go. He wanted to help so badly. The boy wasn't having trouble with his studies alone; he was not well liked. He was intolerant and quickly critical. He had already lost friends in the fraternity. Veras was forced always in his thoughts and musings to return to the enigma: *He says he just doesn't care. Why?*

Joe Miller was another freshman in trouble. Of medium height with dark brown hair, he had eyes that seemed to pop out with curiosity at things that took place around him. Miller's trouble was different than Jennings.'

In the first few weeks his most noteworthy and disarming trait was his ability to prick bubbles of conceit or wistfulness. Miller had all his classes with Staples or me and we could be sent into wild laughter at his observations. Staples had interests and pursuits of his own but Miller and I, both westerners, found many occasions to talk and to laugh.

Once I wrote a theme paper for freshman English. Unsure of my work but wanting it to be good, I took it to Miller for comment. Miller read it and looked up with a twinkle in his remarkable eyes.

"You should be more careful with that stuff," he said.

"Be more careful with what stuff?" I asked.

"Donkey dung."

"What?"

"What, hell," Miller retorted. "Pay attention."

So it went. A time came, though, when Miller no longer attacked the foibles of others, and such times came more and more frequently. He became quieter and less open, preferring after his first weeks to be left alone. I tried to perk him up, teasing or encouraging him.

As the weeks went by, Miller seemed to lose enjoyment even in our friendship and could sometimes be found sitting alone in the library when the rest of the fraternity was studying. Once, finally and to my satisfaction, we talked at length.

The situation was simple: Miller hadn't wanted to come to MIT but his parents had plans for him since birth that included MIT. Now he found he didn't like it.

He had an older brother who had followed his father into engineering. Miller was to do the same, for the family machinery firm in Montana was prosperous and could make use of two sons. Miller, however, wanted no part of the Montana firm. He wanted to be a doctor. He wanted to study liberal arts and go to medical school.

One night just after the first grades came out, Miller came home drunk — his first time. The next morning I teased him as ever but when I found he was seriously depressed, encouraged him to stick it out the rest of the term. Miller wasn't interested.

The following night he went to Jim Veras and asked the house president to drive him to the airport. They talked for several hours and then Miller, without a word of goodbye to anyone, caught a midnight plane to Chicago and home.

Ricardo Haegler studied both at his home in Rio de Janeiro and in Switzerland. This trip to the states was the first extended one for the worldly young man. He pledged Sigma Chi when he learned that a junior in the fraternity, Jose Falcon, was a near neighbor in Rio. Both studied hard enough to stay above the minimum level but no harder. They spent the rest of their time either in sports or in amorous pursuits.

The two of them could describe those pursuits with such vividness that they would soon after starting a tale be surrounded by eager listeners. Miller, before he left, suggested that since the two of them went off together and brought back such lurid tales, what actually happened was that they would fortify themselves with alcohol and, once the edges were fuzzy, begin to imagine their exploits, complementing and enlarging upon each other's story until they were late enough to return as if from a date.

This theory enjoyed wide, laughing circulation until one night both Haegler and Falcon came to the house escorting attractive and attentive young ladies. The theory died a quick death.

Richardo's apparent amorous success plus the fact that many little Americanisms still came too fast or were too colloquial for him made him all the better liked. His responses to unknown words were often charming. He was a popular member of our class of pledges.

William Graham ("Billy") so convinced his roommate he wanted a date for an impending party that his roommate immediately found him a blind date. The roommate didn't know the girl well, and for that matter no one else in the fraternity did either, but she was reputed to wear skirts. To hear Billy talk, skirts were all that was important.

On the night of the party, when the girl appeared, it seemed that Billy wanted something more than skirts. The girl was large, unattractive and unskilled in the ways of college students or in the happenings at college parties. She drank considerably more punch than was good for her and Billy outdrank her two to one.

It was finally arranged, after some difficult times with the two drunk students, that the man who arranged the blind date should take the girl home and I would put Billy to bed.

Billy was loquacious when sober but when drunk the words spilled out in bubbling, cascading torrents. He was too anxious to expound on the terrors of the evening to allow himself to be put in the shower and too determined to relive every moment to dress himself for bed. By the time we finally put him between the blankets of his bunk, his wordiness had drawn an admiring throng.

"Briber," he repeated several times. "Are you there? Did you have a good time tonight? Bob, I've got something to say to you, and just because I'm drunk I don't want you to think it isn't important. It is very important. Whatever you do, Bob, whatever you do, whatever you do, (he started on a fourth repetition but seemed to feel it superfluous) don't ever get drunk. Now, really, Bob, don't laugh. I'm serious. It is not worth it to get drunk. God, I feel terrible. Bob, whatever you do . . . "

I finally succeeded in shooing the crowd out of the room, opened a window and turned out the lights. I assured Billy once more that I would never get drunk and finally the "whatever you do" repetitions slowed down. I snuck out without notice.

Bob Frey bought a slide rule.

A slide rule is an expensive implement and an investment comparable to a good fountain pen. It's a useful, almost essential, device. Buy one for twenty dollars and a man was outfitted for life. Twenty dollars, however, was a lot of money: A typical month of meals and lodging in the fraternity house cost about $100. It was the first real tie the freshman has with his pictured dream world: "The engineer and his slide rule."

Frey made his choice of a slide rule with great care. He devoted a week to deciding. He and I spent a walk across the bridge while he described the intricacies of the model he chose. He carried the slide rule, neatly tucked in its long black case, to a physics quiz. He pictured in glowing terms what his slide rule could do for him. "You just watch, man. I'll hit that quiz!"

Frey and Billy crossed the bridge at lunchtime, returning to the fraternity. Frey had forgotten about the slide rule. He was bemoaning the "silly damn mistake" of multiplying instead of dividing on a question in the physics quiz, a very human mistake. He calculated he had lost at least five and maybe ten points.

He was conjuring up visions of the points he would be graded down, I was told later, when suddenly he paused and gasped. "Jeez! I forgot to take the square root on the last problem!" By now both had stopped. Frey looked stunned. He picked up the slide rule and made as if to throw the cursed thing into the river.

Somehow the end of the black case flew open. The slide rule slipped out and rotating lazily described a tantalizing arc as it sailed gracefully over the water. It splashed gently a few feet from the bridge and slowly wigwagged its way out of sight.

When Frey could tear his eyes from the water, he turned around, pale and weak. He was greeted by a fresh delight: Billy was leaning against the bridge railing, trying to look sympathetic while simultaneously shaking with laughter.

Frey looked at him with agonized eyes and was silent for a moment. Finally he whispered, "Damn. God Damn," and walked on alone.

One of the actives confided to me when six-week grades came out that he had "one terrible time" telling Jerry Laufs and me apart. We were both tall and blond and seemed always to be together. We lived in adjoining rooms. We also both had identical, excellent six week grades. I replied to the comment that "Jerry would be put out if he knew that some couldn't tell us apart," and laughed it off, but it bothered me.

It was true that superficially we had much in common, but I knew of wide differences between Laufs and me. That others didn't see the differences was disquieting. The truth was that I was not terribly fond of my new pledge brother.

One night I finished my studying early and wandered through the house in search of diversion. The game room in the basement was empty. The music room, directly above it, was quiet; a senior, reading the new issue of LIFE magazine wasn't interested in talking even if I could think of something to say. The library was in use by three juniors who decided they finally must work on a marketing report due the next day.

I couldn't find diversion so I had to make my own. Laufs, in his fourth floor room, was just finishing his homework. Here was a likely target for talk. "Finish your work?" I asked.

"Yes, I just completed chemistry," Laufs answered. "I thought the last problem had to be worked using equivalent weights alone, but they really wanted you to use concentrations. I didn't realize it until I looked at tomorrow night's homework."

"Isn't that just like the guy," I thought to myself. "He waits until I finish my work and then he springs tomorrow night's homework on me."

"Yeah, I wondered about that," I said aloud. "I didn't think they would do it to us, though, so I just worked it the old way. What answer'd you get?"

"Here, look." Laufs worked through the problem with the joy of playing with a new toy. He explained his answer slowly and carefully, even pedantically. When he finally turned the page and uncovered his answer, I cut him off.

"Oh, I see," I said, "I didn't think of that."

"How can you see? I haven't finished the problem yet."

"Look, Jerry, you may think I'm slow, but at least I can get along in chemistry."

"I don't think you're slow. Who said that? I just want to work it through from the beginning so I'm sure it's all right."

"You know, that's the difference between you and me," I said. "You work these problems through carefully and you hand in neat, recopied answers. I just do the damn problems and hand 'em in."

The idea that Laufs might feel superior rankled me, so I challenged him. "But I'll bet I end up here with better grades than you."

"Think so? Laufs looked at me quizzically.

"Yes. I'll bet you five bucks I get better grades. We'll be taking the same courses and having the same teachers all the way through. It's a fair bet."

"Well, you go right ahead and get good grades. It'll be good for the fraternity if both of us do well."

"I'll bet you five bucks I do better than you."

"I don't want to bet. Why should I bet? I'll be glad to have you get better grades than I do. I know what I want to do and I'll do it regardless of what you do. And, anyway, I can't afford five dollars."

My temper flared. I was frustrated and wanted a tangible challenge. Here was a person worthy of a challenge who wouldn't take it. *"Damn him anyway, he was just too smug and cool."*

Laufs had told me something of his upbringing, that he had been brought up in a house full of strong-willed women *("one of that kind was a houseful,"* I thought *"but three?")* but he was far from effeminate. Already he had started dating and working out with the freshman crew team. Already he had angered me with his calm determination.

I was feeling for the first time the frustration uncertain ambition feels when it meets complacent ability, but I gradually calmed down. Finally I found myself asking "What do you want, Jerry?"

Laufs, oblivious to the mental maelstrom that had gone on in my mind, answered casually, "I want to be a fine chemical engineer, and I want to learn all the things that are taught. It's too expensive a place not to get everything I can out of it, and I owe it to my folks to get good grades." He looked at me seriously, pleased with his answer.

"What do you want?" he asked.

I hesitated for a moment, deciding whether or not to unburden myself.

"Like what?" Laufs asked.

"Well, like learning how to get along with people and how to get things done. Dad told me I should learn how to think. How to make a speech and how to be an engineer. I want to go into student activities."

"Well, I want to do those things also. But my schoolwork comes first," he responded.

"Oh sure, my schoolwork comes first, but I want to do them all."

I found my diversion. We continued talking about life and dreams until minutes before "lights out" for pledges, 12:30.

When I finally found my bed I reviewed what I had said. It had been a bit uncomfortable to give words to my goals, but once I spoke the words the goals seemed more certain.

First Snow

The first snow came that year on Friday afternoon December first. It fell gently in huge flakes and covered all the dirty gashes of the city with a scar-hiding coverlet of clean white snow.

The snow was still settling when the streetlights came on. People fortunate to be walking through it saw celestial pathways of glitter descend to their eyes from each streetlight they passed as light reflected off the falling snowflakes.

The snow deadened sound as well. Cars passed in sluicing silence. Car horns continued to blare but their cacophony was quieted before it traveled far. Now and then the sharp laughter of a student rang out as his snowball only nearly missed a coed, but even that was a fresh sound, a sound unsullied by familiarity.

The Sigma Chis, and particularly the freshmen, found this snow entirely to their liking. For some Southern freshmen it was the most snow they had ever seen. For others it marked the true beginning of a fresh season. For all it marked a welcome change: schoolwork was wearing thin. Constant assignments and quizzes demanded continued effort. Effort, in turn, demanded relaxation. Here, everywhere, was six inches of readymade relaxation. Excitement was everywhere.

"Go on! Throw it!"

"Ha Ha Ha! You missed! You gotta be better than that."

A snowball fight was in full force. Laufs and I were teamed against Sauer and Billy. The north side of Beacon Street was one fortress, the south side the other. Passing cars were nuisances to be thrown around. Parked cars were, alternatively, barriers for safety or common inconveniences.

"All right, guys! Let's see you match this!" Splutch!

"Oof! Come on Rebel, you don't show me much. Just because you've never seen snow is no cause to be wild!"

"Never seen snow?" Splutch! "All right already. So you used to play left field for the Yankees! Just do it again!"

Dinner that night was boisterous. Song broke out spontaneously, fitting the collegiate environment of the paneled room, but more than one pat of butter found its way into a neighbor's hair; more than one glass of water into his coat pocket. The seniors looked on benignly, sharing mentally since dignity and maturity prevented their sharing physically. Juniors, conscious of their responsibility toward urging the freshmen on and their growing maturity, alternatively cheering or shushing the fight. The sophomores and the freshmen went hard at it.

"Briber, what's the idea of breaking a window?"

"Me? I didn't break a window! Look, dead eye, if you mean dodging a wild throw means hitting a window . . . "

"You guys are both wrong. I saw Laufs hit the window."

"How could I? I was throwing the other way!"

"All right, Jerry. We all know you're not very accurate."

The crowning event of the dinner came when classmates duped Billy into standing and holding a lighted candle aloft while the rest sang "Happy Birthday."

Jennings bet the group two dollars that he would push a piece of pie into Frey's face. Someone accepted for him and Frey, incredulous, pooh-poohed the idea. Jennings passed a hat around, collected the money and did as he had promised. When the money was counted, there was enough not only to pay off the bet but enough left over to clean Frey's coat.

The dining room at the Sigma Chi house. We gathered here in coat and tie for dinner every evening. The phrase in the stained glass window read, "Strive mightily but eat and drink as friends."

After dinner four of us ascended to the graveled roof. The roof door was open and seemed designed to lead to snowball events. Each rolled-up snowball picked up enough gravel to rattle against windows when it was dropped on the sidewalk and exploded four floors below.

We eyed the blue mailbox that stood in front of the fraternity house with interest, but agreed after discussion that squashing a mailbox with a huge snowball would come under the category "tampering with the mail" and would be far more serious than rattling a window or two. Our first snow had effect enough.

"Do You Love Me?"

Every year the fraternity observed a colorful routine. A guy couldn't come to Boston, so the story went, without seeing the Red Sox, hearing the Boston Symphony or visiting the burlesque. Accordingly, each year the seniors chaperoned the freshmen to the burlesque and then for a round of the dives in Scollay Square, Boston's red light district. (Freshmen were on their own for a Red Sox game or the Symphony.) Freshmen would wait their turn and when they were seniors, repeat the routine.

My love interest lay with a high school sweetheart or, as I had to admit, with a high school friend, but after three months away the letters were becoming unsatisfactory. By the time of the fall formal, a week after first snow, I had turned in only a few hours of feminine companionship escorting a senior's younger sister to the movies. It was time to meet a Boston girl.

My first chance came at an acquaintance dance for freshmen at a neighboring womens' college. Acquaintance dances, I heard, were parties of the devil, but they did serve the purpose of thrusting boys and girls together. Six Sigma Chi freshmen and a duty-bound and lonesome junior went to the dance and each thereafter went largely different ways.

Two of the freshmen, Laufs included, and the junior, started dancing immediately and danced all evening. One of the freshmen met a girl he intended to date, but for the others their only stimulation was the exercise. Each danced with at most two of the apparently disinterested girls.

Billy watched for an hour and then barged in on the most popular girl at the dance, only to be cut in on immediately. He returned, bemoaning his misfortune, and spent the remaining hour critiquing. I found a pleasant girl and was evidently well received, for we spent the time either dancing or talking in the gardens. The girl, Phyllis, was attractive. Her deep brown clear eyes and identically colored hair set off a beautiful complexion. Her only distracting feature and one which may have influenced my reception were very obvious buck teeth. At any rate she was clever and pleasant and before I left I had arranged a date for the following weekend's beach party.

Spirits were high as we returned from the beach. I was a bit inebriated and Phyllis was in the best of spirits. Two couples crowded into the back seat of the car and the only solution, everyone agreed, each girl sat on her date's lap. The opportunity was too good to miss. I kissed her. The kiss was still in process, however, when I began giggling.

"What's the matter?" Phyllis broke free immediately.

"Oh. . . Ah. . I was just thinking of the way we threw Sauer into the water."

"This is a terrible time to be thinking of that," she said sharply. I thought a minute and decided she had better just remain perturbed. I pulled her closer and kissed her again.

The similarity between kissing her and eating an ear of corn took me completely by surprise. Better by far to kiss her again and let her be mad at me for laughing at a thought than to hurt her by telling her the real reason.

We parted coolly. I could never summon up nerve enough to face her again.

A friend, George Dickson, arranged my next time spent with female companionship. It would be, Dickson said, "a blind date. Now, ha ha, don't get the idea that I mean she would come in with a police dog in a harness. Ha Ha. Really, Bob, she's a lot of fun."

I was interested and let the description stop there. I hadn't learned yet that there was a distinction between a nice girl and a girl who is a "lot of fun" or between either and a "good looker." There were no doubt girls who had two or three of these characteristics at one time, but the characteristic I met this time was a "lot of fun."

The date started out calmly enough with a simple trip to Wellesley, a soft drink, and a walk around campus.

George drove us out in his huge old black car and the trip out and introductions went smoothly. Mary Halloran was tall and thin and pleasantly proportioned. Her face was old for the face of a college freshman, but pleasant. She had a sense of humor and was the promised "lots of fun."

The rest of the first evening was spent in innocuous pursuits. The talk was of hometowns and studies and the rambling, almost medieval, Wellesley campus. It was not until nearly sign-in time for the dates that the girl and I were alone.

The talk turned to personalities and goals and ambitions. Hers was simply to be a mother, mine to be the so-far undefined success, hopefully to be an important person on campus.

Little intimacies encouraged me. Mary let her hand be held; she didn't remove my arm from around her as we passed a streetlight and walked in shadows to the next. Finally, almost without effort, I kissed her.

The drive home was long and quiet. It was late and streetlights accentuated the coldness of empty stores we passed. The streets were empty. We were nearly home when Dickson spoke.

"Did you have a good time?"

"I don't know." I wasn't used to kissing a girl on the first serious date; I couldn't decide whether it was good or bad. Years of repressed dating and earlier values colored my reaction. "Good or bad?" I didn't know.

"I had a great time," Dickson said. "I always have a good time on a date. The girl is really a queen."

"You're right. She's a real peach. What year is she?"

"She's a junior. She's not very good looking but I always liked the pudgy ones. There's no chance of losing them in the dark." Dickson broke into his raucous, infectious laugh and then paused. "She and Mary seem to get along very well."

"Yeah. Both are taking history and Mary thinks a lot of your girl," I said.

"Are you going to take her out again?" Dickson asked.

"Who?"

"Who, nuts. Face it, man, you've got no choice. Mary."

"Oh, I don't know. We'll see . . . you know, that campus is a beautiful place."

About a week later events forced a decision. The fraternity's annual fall formal, our "Autumn Triad," was only two weeks away and I didn't have a date. When Dickson and Johnny Harris, my roommate, discovered this they were irreconcilable. "Briber, face it, you've got to get a date. The Triad is a weekend party that everybody goes to. You've just got to get a date."

"Oh, I'll get a date."

"When?"

"Tomorrow."

"Tomorrow hell, "Dickson said. "There's no time like right now. Go get a date."

"Who with? You guys have got me wrong. I'm really a peaceful-type engineer. I don't fool around with these wild women."

"Who said anything about wild women?"

"She'd have to be wild to go out with me."

"Oh, come on. You're just saying that cause it's true," Dickson laughed.

My friends left me no choice. Harris and Dickson decided the best plan would be to lock me in a phone booth until I got a date. They gave me a dime and waited in the library. When finally they released me they were both genuinely surprised that I had a date. Mary Halloran said she was "happy to go, Bob."

"Happy to go" made me vaguely uncomfortable. Not "I'd be delighted," or even a simple "Yes," but "Happy to go." *"Was she doing me a favor?"*

Twice a year, for weekend parties, the Sigma Chis arranged their affairs sufficiently to invite the women to move into the fraternity house and they went to find lodging wherever they could, on the floor of a friend's room, home, wherever.

Friday night the party started with cocktails, a big banquet and a formal dance. Saturday afternoon (no one bothered to be up on Saturday morning) everyone gathered to decorate the fraternity house for an informal dance and a party. Sunday morning a nearby church offered services some attended, and Sunday afternoon a false-bearded, pillow-enlarged brother, sporting an incongruous southern accent, emerged to present gifts and corny jokes to all. Finally the weekend ended with much hand holding and sad goodbyes, couples usually to be apart for at least a week.

Mary and I got along well enough Friday evening, even though I dropped a drink at the cocktail party and Mary showed aggravating interest in an undated junior. The formal banquet was uneventfully completed and dancing began. The affection which dancing together can bring, however, just didn't show up for us.

Finally, at the Saturday night party, Mary insisted we leave the dance and make the rounds of other fraternity parties. Highball followed highball, quick dance followed dance and finally there was nothing to do but go back to the Sigma Chi house.

The library at 2 am was dark but not empty. Mary and I went in amid loud demands that we shut the door behind us. We identified who was sitting where and found an empty chair. Somewhat uncomfortably we settled in.

I felt her body pressing on mine and, after a few murmured comments, kissed her. She kissed me in return.

After a quiet spell of ardor, Mary looked at me in the dim light.

"Bob, do you love me?"

I woke as if from a dream. "What did you say?"

"You love me, don't you?"

"No, I don't love you."

The girl sat up, straight and stiff.

"After what we've just done, you've got to love me."

"Why?"

"I'm ruined if you don't."

"Ruined, hell! You haven't even been touched."

"I don't like you."

"That's interesting. Why don't you like me?"

"You're too efficient. I'm not your kind at all. I'm a homebody and some-day I'll be a mother and a housewife. You're too cold."

"I'll agree you're not my kind. We don't get along very well, that's for sure, but I'm not cold. Did I act cold tonight?"

"Well, no. But you're too ambitious and efficient."

I liked to think I was efficient — what was wrong with that? — but what had I done at a dance to appear "too ambitious and efficient ?" I was mystified.

"And besides, you don't even want to get married."

"Who said I didn't want to get married?"

"You give me that idea."

"How?"

"Oh, I don't know. You just do."

The fraternity had to be cleared of all the brothers by 3 am. The disagree-ment between me and my unhappy date was brought to a halt by curfew.

The next morning Mary asked to borrow three dollars to take a taxi home. She left shortly before noon. I was not sorry to see her off.

We End a Term

The first college term ended in January unheralded by weather. Gray day followed gray day. Snow fell about once a week but its freshness was gone. It fell and for a while the piles of unmelted snow assumed the dimensions of minor mountains, but soot fell even more relentlessly and the mysterious mountains were once again shown to be just mounds of dirty snow.

Most Sigma Chi freshmen had finished one term and were starting a second. Six of our original pledge class remained; two were gone. Joe Miller flew home in the night, quietly and without comment; Tom Jennings flunked out much as he had come, with a spurt of forced good fellowship and a borrowed cigarette.

Whose fault the departures? The impression that their son is prepared always persists, and adoring parents send their son away to college with kisses and much fondness but not much else: "There goes our fine son to challenge the wide world." He goes proudly and returns defeated.

Those staying in Boston devoted two days between terms to painting and cleaning. A room that had been battleship gray two years ago blossomed into canary yellow last year and now into a pale pastel green. The more important change, though, came in the people. The seniors had completed seven terms; the freshmen their first. The borderline course was flunked or passed — but it was over and an accomplishment for all.

"Jim?" Billy called. Jim Veras, fraternity president, stood on the front steps of the fraternity house, watching the cab that carried Tom Jennings away, no doubt for the last time. Several of us joined in watching. Veras, though, was lost in thought and regrets. He had tried hard to keep Jennings in school.

"Jim Veras! VERAS!" Billy called again. "Why are you standing there staring at traffic? Thinking about some woman is not worth freezing for. Go inside! Try thinking of her inside. It's great what warmth can do for sex."

Veras turned, his chain of thought broken. Tom Jennings was gone.

"Oh, hi, Billy."

"When do house rules go off? I'm in the mood for a beer."

"You can get a beer at the corner. You don't have to wait for house rules to go off for that."

"I know, but I'd rather have it here in the house."

"Well, the last final exam was today. They're off now." Veras was the authority.

"That's great!" Billy turned and walked rapidly down the street. Now that house rules were relaxed, as every vacation they were, he would be free to drink in the house or, maybe, even take a woman above the second floor. Billy hadn't had such an opportunity, but he could fantasize.

His walk, as he hurried toward the source of beer, showed resolve that he seldom showed when he went to class. Veras smiled wanly as the chubby freshman disappeared and turned to pack for his own vacation in New York City.

Billy returned a few minutes later, bearing a thick smile and a six-pack of cold beer, prepared to violate his own forgotten injunction: "Whatever you do, Bob, whatever . ."

The fraternity house showed all the signs of a complete release in tension. Clothes were strewn on banisters that were kept bare earlier. Magazines were scattered throughout the library and the music room. A third of the members had left for elsewhere, but their goodbyes were not the goodbyes of final farewell such as that between the house president and Tom Jennings. Most would be back in a few days.

In the library, three of us with no home to go to and no classes to attend were immersed in conversation. "Bob Frey, how soon are you going to see Lefty?" I asked.

"Tomorrow night. We've got a date to go dancing. Damn, that's going to be good stuff. It's been eighteen days since I've seen her."

"When did you write last?"

"Last night."

"How often do you write?"

"Every day." Frey seemed a little embarrassed by the admission, and his admission immediately solicited the attention of George Dickson. He put down his magazine and chuckled.

"Frey, I'll bet you a steak dinner you don't keep that up beyond the end of next term. I've never seen a freshman that did."

"Oh, I don't know," Frey said. "I've written her every day since I came here." Several of us listened without comment. I had intended to write a girl from home at least twice a week but I fit the mold Dickson cast. The letters slowed before a month had passed and now I felt lucky to get a letter.

"You seem crazy about this girl, Bob. Why don't you get pinned?" Dickson was in a teasing mood and Frey's situation made him good bait.

"I can't get pinned. I don't have a pin. All I've got is a pledge button."

"You don't have to have a pin. You can give her your pledge button if you stick to the rules. A long and dignified tradition," and here Dickson put on his most pompous, all-knowing air, "has it that you can give a girl a pledge button, if you meet just one small condition. You've got to pin it to her brassiere."

His ludicrous pedantry delighted us all. We wanted more. "How are you going to prove you gave it to her? She'll put her clothes on over the pin," someone asked.

"Naturally. Need you ask? How else do you suppose she could show it off?"

The idea didn't appeal to Frey, and his brow furled as he said, "but the pledge button is not like the fraternity pin. It hasn't got a pin — it's got a thing you've got to screw on to make it stick. That means you've got to be inside the — well, you can't just stick it on."

Dickson's face contorted with delight; this had gone better than expected. "Well," he said, "what's a little obstacle like that in the way of true love?" Finally he could hold it no longer and bellowed forth his raucous laughter.

Frey tried to break in, but couldn't be heard. He decided to retire from the field. His parting comment as he left the room, "Well, anyway, we're not ready to get pinned," made Dickson laugh even harder.

Hell Week

A pin, however, was not long in coming to Bob Frey or any of the other freshmen, except those lost to MIT.

The freshmen spent their first term in vassalage with duties and classes run by a fraternity brother. One freshman was older even than some seniors due to a tour of Army duty and subservience didn't wear well with him, but all were glad to see it end. We had learned to respect the privileges of active membership without being exposed to many of its tribulations.

The disappearance of all the active brothers to regular Monday night "chapter meetings" created an aura of mystery and desirability to active membership. Just as the new bride may be told never to appear in the altogether before her new husband but always to wear a shimmering black bit of something, so the freshmen had been kept away from savoring the things that someday might lose their allure. Presumably their allegiance had now been secured and the right to wear the fraternity pin would be the next step.

Though none of the freshmen would talk with an active about that next step, the so-called "right of passage," it was a common topic among them. They talked about Hell Week at length.

Tales were told of duties imposed by some fraternities. Eating dinner without utensils or walking across the Harvard Bridge balanced on tin cans strapped to a pledge's shoes were among the least odious. Perhaps 5,000 balusters support the railings of the Harvard Bridge and to tie a string on each on a cold and windy night would be a miserable job even for a pledge class of eight or ten, especially if they knew the strings were to be cut off the following night. To secure an autographed brassiere from the current feature performer at the burlesque could be difficult. Perhaps they would be required to carry mouthfuls of slop down three flights of stairs, on hand and knee, to put out a frequently-banked fire in the living room fireplace. Such merely unpleasant tales made the rounds of the pledges; others described heinous requirements, even leading in one later year at another fraternity to fatality. Hell Week was viewed with a mixture of dread and anticipation.

The freshmen, however, had earned the right at last to be free of subjugation. Bob Frey, even with writing his girl every night, found time to play in a football game organized by the Institute for the freshmen to play the sophomores, and to keep up with his studies using a borrowed slide rule.

Billy managed to pass. Billy was one with shifting allegiances toward older students. His primary allegiance for the latter part of the first term settled on an unquestionably brilliant senior. Somewhat unpredictable in his ways, the senior would disappear for a week at a time, missing class, bed and board, only to reappear suddenly and devote himself to continuous study. A very bright (though mercurial) guy, he earned just short of straight "A" grades in a college in which that was very unusual.

Billy copied the antics of this senior in his own freshman version and disappeared for two days just before final exams. When he reappeared, he carefully gave the appearance that he planned to study full time until he passed his exams. We had to wake him up at his desk two mornings in a row. It speaks well of an idol Billy admired earlier in the term, who followed up with careful, thoughtful tutoring, that Billy didn't follow Tom Jennings out the door.

Ricardo Haegler, the Brazilian with the penchant for women or, at least, for stories of women, did well enough. On his weekdays he studied diligently and came through satisfactorily.

I ended the term with grades second only to Laufs and, in keeping with my ambitions, made friends across campus as well.

Other changes resulted from a change of mind. I changed my major course of study from chemical engineering to business with a minor in chemical engineering. That way I could spend more time in extracurricular pursuits and less time in laboratories.

I learned in those pursuits about bylaws, budgets and meetings, and about MIT's method of supporting student affairs. I met people in the faculty and administration — men mostly, for women were uncommon — and met many students other than fraternity brothers. All of this stood well for me a year or two later when student elections filled my spare time, but now I prepared for Hell Week.

We found out right away what this passage, this "Hell Week," meant to us: no heinous or ridiculous assignments, just work. Much of the week, after study and before an abnormally late bedtime, we cleaned and repaired the common rooms of the fraternity house.

The week ended with a solemn ceremony telling us what Sigma Chi meant to its members and even teaching us our fraternity's "secret" handshake. The assembled crowd then greeted us with warm congratulations all around. Finally we really belonged.

Now I was even freer to work in student affairs. By my junior year I was ready to run for class office, and with friends had planned a campaign. I had made something of a name in the fraternity world by running a competitive, successful pledge drive in my junior year. We had pledged an unusually large number of freshmen that year, as every fraternity tried to do.

My fraternity brothers chose me to host, for an abbreviated weekend, the national "Sweetheart of Sigma Chi" as she visited various campuses with a chapter of the fraternity, I got a bit of local publicity for a pleasant weekend. I believed that much of the fraternity world would vote for me, anyway, just to vote against a dormitory resident.

**Friends help me welcome the "Sweetheart of Sigma
Chi" to our fraternity for a weekend party.**

"Fifty-two together," we called our slate of candidates because it included both fraternity members and dorm residents. We spent our time until the election making posters, sitting in a busy corridor talking with anyone who would listen, and now and then knocking on dormitory doors. And then it was over.

The Election

"Bob, congratulations. You've won!"

"I've won? How do you know?"

"I was over counting ballots. It was close for a while but you won by about fifty votes."

I couldn't quite comprehend. I looked about the paneled library at the dozen of my fraternity brothers who returned the look, expressions of congratulations forming on their faces.

I turned to question my informant, Al Ward. A doubt arose. "Do you think there is any chance the counting was wrong? I mean, have they checked it?"

Al Ward brushed aside the concern. "Well, I didn't stay around for the final check but there was no question in anyone's mind. I wanted to get over to the house to tell you."

I leaned back against the large brown leather couch, startled by the suddenness with which the weeks of intense activity ended. It didn't seem possible to have been so tied up with an election campaign and so thoroughly immersed in its intrigues to have it all end so abruptly. But Al Ward said, "You've won." I was to be the President of my Senior Class, Chairman of the student government's "Institute Committee," and, in short, Mr. MIT Student Government.

"No, that couldn't be right! The President of the Senior Class was always someone else, someone you admired from a distance. He was the man who spoke to the freshmen

at their orientation program and his classmates at graduation, who hobnobbed with the President, who . . ."

But Al Ward said, "Bob, you've won." After a pause I jumped up, almost shrieking, "I've won! I've won!" I slapped Al Ward on the back with such violence that that he reeled forward. "Al, I've won!"

"I'm glad you heard me. I was worried about you there for a minute." The tension in the room was broken. Fraternity brothers rushed forward.

"Ole Sigma Chi really has a rushing asset now," said one. "The President of the Senior Class will really wow the freshmen!" said another. The hubbub went on for twenty minutes.

"I hate to tell you guys this," I broke in, "but I'll be living in a dorm room next year. MIT gives the President of the Senior Class free board and room. I guess they want to get at me easily. I'll be living across the bridge."

I thought of that train station departure years before and of the many phone calls and letters since. I went downstairs to call my parents.

;

A Gun, a Panty Raid
and a Communist
1952

Student Body President

So what do you win when you win the job of Senior Class President? The MIT Senior Class President becomes Student Body President and chairs the student legislature, the "Institute Committee" known by its abbreviation "Ins Comm." The role usually asked ordinary things of me: I ran meetings, worked on class events, studied bylaws and budgets, and often just answered questions. Occasionally I would be called upon to speak out for, or to, the student body privately as at a meeting or publicly as at graduation.

I was busy doing mostly routine things, but unusual events did happen. Once in a while I enjoyed the small glory of knowing some people thought class presidents were important, including a date or two. It was a fun job and the challenges were noteworthy.

Ins Comm was organized around 25 representatives of classes and organizations, with an Executive Committee and a normal roster of officers and class officials. Both the Secretary and the Treasurer (my brother had been Treasurer nine years earlier) also headed committees concerned with their role. We adhered as best we could to parliamentary rules of order that included seeing that minutes of meetings were written, approved and stored. A friend called me the "fastest minutes-reader ever" because as Chairman I read them aloud at Ins Comm meetings.

MIT treated its student government well. We were given $50,000 a year to spend on student activities, quite a lot of money at the time. MIT also paid athletic expenses such as salaries, uniforms and travel, and paid the salary of a secretary who worked both for me and for Ins Comm. We spent our money on many clubs and organizations, such as a model railroad club, a debating society, a Chinese students' club, student branches of professional societies and other groups, most needing a little money. After giving us that money and being expected to spend and keep track of it, MIT pretty much left us alone.

I moved to a dormitory room and looked across the Charles River at the backs of the fraternity houses on Beacon Street. Commuting became a matter of traveling back across the Harvard Bridge for fraternity meetings and parties. I had a full new life directly on campus.

Late in the school year this generous hands-off attitude toward student government changed. We had a mechanism in place to discuss normal student concerns, a secret society called *"Osiris"* which brought fifteen students together periodically with faculty and administrators for a cordial dinner and conversation.

Suddenly these meetings became insufficient. A different level of concern showed up when a fearsome issue exploded on campus and student government had an important role in dealing with it.

Noteworthy events preceded that explosion, however, and kept the job interesting.

"I Am Afraid for My Life"

I described one event in a letter to my parents that read about as follows, using politically correct words and descriptions that I felt wouldn't distress them. I wasn't completely accurate about alcohol, for instance, or say why the girl was on the bed in her slip.

"Tuesday night, about 10:30, I got a call from Jay Koogle, junior, who lives in a nearby dormitory," I wrote. "I thought of him as a very clear thinking kid, though Fred Fassett (close friend and Faculty Resident in my dormitory) told me he thinks Jay's 'a little ego-centric.'

"'Bob,' Jay said on the phone, 'I don't want to appear sensationalistic, but right now I am afraid for my life.'" His story unfolded.

"About three weeks before, Jay and his roommate Mike had a double date, and Mike, being a very insistent chap, brought unusual events to the evening. Nobody had been drinking, (I wrote) but Mike finally managed to take a picture of his date on his bed with only her slip on. The girl is young and very flighty and it was all above board," I wrote my parents, "but it was an incriminating photo.

"Well, Mike later threatened the girl with the pictures because he wanted to make sure she still went out with him. The girl called Jay, explained the situation, and asked Jay to get rid of the pictures. Jay told Mike that she wanted the pictures destroyed and he would destroy them himself if Mike didn't. Well, Mike didn't, so Jay tore them up.

"Later than night Mike came in with a 25 caliber pistol, threatened Jay, said he would kill him, and tapped him playfully in the face with the gun.

"Things cooled off that night but the next night when Mike came in he seemed to be in a real stew. Jay thought he heard him go into his room, pick up the pistol and root around for shells. He then went into Jay's room.

"When Jay heard all this he ducked out and went down a fire escape to the faculty residence in his dormitory. The Faculty Resident wasn't around, so he called me. I called Fred Fassett and asked him to stay around in case the Dean of Students or other help wasn't available, and went to retrieve Jay. After frantically looking around for the Dean or other support, Jay and I went to the Fassett's residence.

"We finally located the missing Dean and Faculty Resident and phone calls flew between the two Faculty Residents and the Dean of Students. Jay ended up spending the night at the Fassett's.

"The next morning both Faculty Residents, the Dean and a couple others closeted themselves with Mike for two hours and really ran him up and down. They were set to expel him on the spot but the Dean, also a trained psychiatrist, said, 'No, give me a chance.' That's about how things stand now. Jay is back in his room, he and Mike are on speaking terms, and Mike is spending time with the Dean/psychiatrist."

With that momentary fright, a hurried campus search and then relative peace, the issue disappeared. To this day I don't know how much Jay exaggerated or how much of the threat was true. I didn't write about it again.

The Dean Incites a Riot

Fred Fassett and his wife Julie were close friends. They introduced me to my first wife and encouraged the nascent relationship. I read the first draft of "On Crossing Harvard Bridge" to them. They encouraged me to continue with it and in other ways filled my senior year and the following ones when I worked for the Institute with a friendly, familial relationship.

Fred came to his job at MIT, I believe, because Dr. Killian, MIT president, knew him in Washington, DC, where he was involved in publications for a government agency. Fred loved books, in part just for what they were and in part because they, more than the newspapers or TV he detested, represented the kind of refined and educated world he loved. Fred and Julie were stylish role models for MIT students, often the first generation in their family to go to college. I suspect Dr. Killian brought Fred to Cambridge for just that reason.

Fred had worked in a print shop as a young man and progressed to the role of publisher. He showed me "edge-printed" books (the book is closed and text is applied to the cut edges, like gilt-edging the pages but with printed words), which I had never seen. He talked with great excitement about forthcoming computer technology, where the size and even the font of a typeface could be changed without laboriously setting rack after rack of type.

The love of books and photographs, and discussing them, had been his life. He was a wonderful and widely experienced foil for the sometimes nerdy MIT students.

Fred loved to talk books and photography and made wonderful conversation. A small man with salt-and-pepper hair, he spoke in a cultured, almost British way, his tie and coat in careful order and his words chosen and pronounced with care. As a young man he had lost the two smaller fingers on his right hand, so shaking hands with him was like picking up a teacup.

Julie was a fitting mate. Both were State-of-Mainers but Julie showed it more. She was outspoken and frank but also loving and supportive. They moved from the Faculty residence in our dormitory to a grand Dean's house where she organized and held many Sunday afternoon receptions for students. She wanted to invite every MIT undergraduate to a reception, and went about it dorm floor by dorm floor, fraternity by fraternity. Whether or not she invited them all, she certainly brought many students to many classy Sunday afternoon affairs, in her ambitious attempt to bring manners, and maybe even culture, to MIT students.

Fred loved to talk with students almost as much, I think, as he loved his evening martini or two to go with the conversation. He had a rigid formula for the drink: 4 parts gin, 1 part vermouth and 1 part water, on ice with an olive. He loved the drink, especially when he reached the last precious drops: "Cat pee" he called them.

Then one evening things changed.

Daylight savings time in the spring brings an extra hour of evening light to campuses just as it does to farms. The time change may affect students almost as much as it does farmers. Suddenly, after months of cold and dismal early darkness, days stay bright an extra hour and the weather often turns warm. Students who studied strenuously from dinner time through the evening suddenly find an hour of freedom. Warmth and light replaces cold and dark, and what's more, the school year is drawing to a close. The change can bring celebration.

Students in my dormitory celebrated boisterously on one Monday night in May. They built a roaring fire in our athletic field, threw balloons full of water out windows, even putting up a fake "detour" sign in the road to force cars to drive under the windows. They set off fireworks. They raised hell enough to rouse the police and fire departments.

Fred and Julie Fassett at my 1956 wedding in Philadelphia

Had the police and firemen never come, I don't believe the caravan to Radcliffe would ever have started. Having the law around just added a challenge to the celebration. (Radcliffe was chosen because it was the nearest target for a "panty raid," said to honor some girl somewhere who threw a pair out her window to a boisterous bunch below.) But the caravan did start and it ended poorly. The police called it a "riot." Nineteen students were jailed with the prospect that they would be charged with "disturbing the peace."

Fred Fassett left his parlor and second martini and went outdoors to quell the celebration, smelling of alcohol, his glasses and tie askew. He couldn't stop or even dim the ruckus. When the students were carted off to the police station he followed, to try to free or if necessary to bail them out. The next morning the police claimed to newspaper reporters that Fassett was drunk, that he had been dropping water bags out of dormitory windows, and that he incited the students to go to Radcliffe. The newspapers loved the story. It made headlines in Boston and then in New York.

Arraignment was scheduled for a week later.

MIT mustered its defenses and quickly went to Fassett's help. He was cleared of all charges, charges against the students were dismissed, and our attentions turned elsewhere. The event joined the fabled tales that make college life memorable. "College Dean Leads Panty Raid!" said one headline.

The event became a funny tale for many, but never for Fred Fassett. He considered himself a capable publisher and fine Associate Dean, and he was a moderately well-known man. It infuriated him to read the complete falsehood of his role in headline after headline in the newspapers he detested. Even worse, he could do nothing about it.

Students, friends and acquaintances called from all over the country to commiserate, to learn the true facts, whatever. It was a funny story and they wanted to share the joke with him.

The phone calls just extended the unpleasantness for Fred. All he wanted was to forget the whole sorry mess. I spent one evening in his residence answering phone calls so that he and Julie could have some peace, maybe enough for a good night's sleep. I have never felt sorrier for a man.

MIT… a Communist Front?

President Jim Killian and I had a different relationship than might normally be true of a Student Body President and the President of the college. He had been a Sigma Chi at MIT and we saw him at the fraternity
house occasionally in his role as an alumnus. I studied the same Business
Management program at MIT he had studied years before. I dated his daughter Carolyn ('Kit') and for a brief time flirted with a more serious relationship.
I spent some social time with his family, including one lovely Thanksgiving
dinner. Later events in this tale were built upon a base of cordial relationship.

Our relationship, however, was tested over one event.

The year, 1952, was the height of the storm of controversy stirred up by
Senator Joseph McCarthy and the House UnAmerican Affairs Committee
(HUAC). Winds from it blew across the MIT campus. Dr. Dirk J. Struik,
a Dutchman educated in Europe and now professor of mathematics at MIT,
was accused of being a communist. He was indicted for advocating the overthrow of the state and Federal governments. Newspapers and news media
all over the country headlined the issue, with variants of "MIT Professor a
communist."

The MIT community went wild with controversy. All I could gather
was a sense of community confusion, dismay and concern, anger and fear.
Struik himself was uncommunicative, reminding all that he had tenure and
was entitled to his point of view. The stress and controversy around the issue
became as palpable as thunder.

Student government, Ins Comm, would normally not be involved in such an issue, except this time we were. Two students showed up in our offices one day wanting to use our bulletin boards and meeting rooms for publicity and organizational meetings, to build campus-wide support for Struik. It was an ordinary request and we usually granted such privileges. Initially Burge Jamieson, the Secretary to Ins Comm and head of the committee that oversaw facilities use, said "sure, go ahead and get organized."

But this was an unusual organization, and it was sailing under political colors we weren't used to.

These students wanted to organize "Students for Struik," a student group intended to support the well-loved but now suspended professor. They wanted to raise money for his legal defense, to publicize their support and affection for the man and to enlist students all over campus to their cause. The petitioning students argued that their case was justified. After all, we were schooled in the belief that a person is innocent until proven guilty. They felt the HUAC attacks and legal charges made it necessary to come to Struik's defense.

My initial reaction to their request was "hold the phone!" and asked that they be stalled. No luck; they came back and forced the issue. MIT students, as many college students elsewhere, were strong-willed and resolutely skeptical of authority.

When they pressed their case for Struik I wanted to take some time before we granted any such privileges. I wanted to talk it over with the President, for more than just the student government was involved. I felt we had to consider the group in the context of the whole college and I needed to be prepared before "Students for Struik" and their request appeared as an item on the agenda of an Ins Comm meeting.

The media lost no time in announcing that MIT student government was involved, perhaps because in their search for support the group had sought newspaper publicity. The student newspaper, "The Tech," spread the subject all over its front page. Normally student politics are of less interest to the general public than are newspaper pages of tiny legal notices, but this was important. Here was a new actor on a local stage involved in a national headline-grabbing subject. This was newsworthy.

The story seemed to offer evidence about the influence of communists in higher education. We could imagine the world asking: "Are MIT students 'commies,' 'left-wingers,' 'right thinking Americans,' or what?" "Do they support a communist, and how does the college itself feel?"

We were not prepared for such attention, and some of us imagined the worst: "Would we ourselves be called communists or communist sympathizers?" "Could we be indicted for something?" Suddenly our student government and its processes were cast publicly into the middle of the McCarthy storm. We had a hot potato in our hands.

My plan to ask Dr. Killian took a dramatic turn. He asked if our Executive Committee could meet with him, the Dean of Students and a few others at his home on campus at 7:30 the following evening, a day before the pivotal Ins Comm meeting, to talk about the case. I agreed and called an emergency meeting for 7:00 pm, so we could collect ourselves before we met with Dr. Killian and the others. Without knowing more, Burge Jamieson, the Ins Comm Secretary, now reversed his position and denied the group the use of our facilities.

Dr. Killian's request was direct involvement by the MIT administration in our affairs, far beyond anything we had known before. Heretofore we had been free to do pretty much what we wanted but now we were in a public arena much larger than our student world. We were meeting privately with the President and the Dean of Students! We'd never had a meeting solely with the President or Dean of Students on any matter. Most of us had never even been in the President's house.

We were ushered into the large living room of his home on campus at 7:30 that Tuesday evening. The dark room seemed as big as a carpeted basketball court, with here and there softly lit islands of sofas and chairs. We were seated comfortably in one of the islands of light and the meeting began.

The five young students and the one WWII veteran, Ins Comm Vice President Harold Lawrence, were intimidated. Our entire Executive Committee was there, as was the President of the Institute, its Dean of Students and an Assistant to the President. My opponent in the election for class President, Nick Melissas, wasn't a member of the Executive Committee, and so wasn't there. He was at the larger Ins Comm meeting the next day, however, and would have important influence.

Dr. Killian told us after introductions that he would abide by the Institute Committee's decision. He started with that and went on to talk about attention from the press. How do we issue the statement we knew they would want, and how do we keep the press out of the meeting itself? We talked about parliamentary procedure and how to debate the matter. We talked openly, and we touched on many of the elements of recognizing such a student group.

Dr. Killian did not tell us what we should do; he even seemed grateful that we were so concerned. He pointed out many of the difficulties involved in the decision, including the fact that the MIT Faculty Council, speaking for the faculty, advised that it would be deeply unfortunate if such a group were formed. It would be very embarrassing to MIT's position of strict neutrality. He also felt that negative publicity could affect how people felt about MIT students and about MIT itself.

We talked at some length, Dr. Killian gave us his best wishes and we left. It was clear that our attitude had hardened. We were worried about recognizing "Students for Struik" before the meeting, but now we were staunchly opposed. We felt there was too much at stake and too much possible collateral damage if we recognized such a student organization. Fairness to a faculty member, neutrality, or the "innocent until proven guilty" concerns were subjects not relevant in a student debate. The public perception of MIT was.

All we had to do was to convince the larger, complete Institute Committee how right we were when they met the next afternoon. That turned out not to be so easy.

Ins Comm came to order in normal fashion but the meeting went much longer than usual. Close to 100 people filled the room, three or four times the normal crowd. Feelings and noise ran high.

I felt my job was to remain impartial, to be sure everyone had a chance to speak and to bring the group to a decision. I left it to the other members of our Executive Committee to defend our conviction that we should deny privileges to "Students for Struik."

Arguments went back and forth vigorously. Some comments were relevant and some were not: "How should student government deal with student support for an MIT professor charged with advocating the overthrow of the government?" "How can we be neutral to a group that supports him?" "Does academic freedom include the right to advocate overthrowing the government?" "How does 'Students for Struik' fit in with other student clubs and organizations?" "What do we tell the press?" and on and on. An intense three hours later we came to an answer.

Thanks to Nick Melissas we finally reached an effective solution. As is so common in such controversies, the solution was a compromise. This time he suggested it.

The key to compromise was the temporary nature of the group. Melissas argued that Struik would be judged in time; either he would be convicted or absolved of the charges. He was either guilty or innocent. "Students for Struik," as a student organization, would probably have no permanent value in either case.

Other student activities didn't have that temporary nature; they wouldn't succeed or fail based on the results of a trial. The purpose of a student club or activity was essentially permanent, to be appended to their education and to provide a specific experience for interested students. Ordinary student organizations would change only in who was involved, as students progressed from freshmen to seniors and graduation.

So we voted to grant the group "conditional status" until we could see their bylaws, membership, and purpose. Did they intend to serve a longer term purpose than just to help finance one impending trial? Were they committed to that man and his cause, or for something greater? We needed to know some answers and we wanted to grant them the time to prepare answers.

Because he asked me to, I called Dr. Killian as soon as the meeting was over. I was still reeling from the meeting and its intense discussions. We had granted the group conditional recognition, something we had never done before, and we were going to follow them carefully. We wanted bylaws, the names of their officers and an outline of their plans. I told Dr. Killian that

I thought ours was a good decision and fit well with the idea of a neutral approach to a controversial subject.

I wasn't prepared for his response. "Oh," he said disparagingly, "Thank you," and hung up. I was devastated.

Two Boston newspapers followed the story. The Boston Herald did not send a reporter to our meeting but apparently relied on a news service for their information, which in turn must have come from an interpretation of the action we took. They reported we had granted recognition.

A reporter from the Boston Globe waited the three hours outside our meeting room. Hal Lawrence, the Ins Comm Vice President, took the reporter aside and told him of the result of the meeting. Hal could speak with authority; he was Vice President and the President was off doing something else.

He told the reporter how unusual our decision was, that usually we would vote up or down on recognition, usually "yes." In this case we really voted "you're on hold," not quite "no," but we denied use of our facilities until they met various conditions.

The reporter apparently heard that we had refused recognition to "Students for Struik." Hal was himself deeply opposed to recognition of the group so I suspect that was the message he wanted the reporter to hear.

The next morning the two newspapers carried quite different stories. The Boston Herald headline: "Student Group at MIT Wins Recognition." The Boston Globe reported: "Group for Struik at Tech Refused Right to Organize."

I posted both stories outside my door with Scotch tape and added a banner of my own: "Which Paper Do You Read?"

The MIT newspaper, "The Tech," reported the story in detail. Usually they were critical or at least skeptical about Ins Comm activities, but this time was different. The last sentence of their editorial read: "To those who are afraid of the consequences of the decision made by the Institute Committee, we would say this: 'As long as Technology continues to send out into the world the type of men who sat on Ins Comm last Wednesday, men who will grant free expression to opinions completely different from their own, there is no danger that the good name of the Institute will suffer."

After the meeting several people wanted to force reconsideration of the decision. At least two members of our Executive Committee still wanted to deny use of our facilities. Burge Jamieson, our Secretary, was writing down the names of the petitioners when the leader of "Students for Struik" snatched the list from Burge. "Well," he said ominously, holding the list, "now we will have to go underground." He later said that he was just joking.

That evening I had a phone conversation with the group leader. He said he didn't trust Burge Jamieson and didn't understand what was going on. "Why was he taking our names?" I explained that we needed the names for our records, that it was part of our decision. After we talked for forty-five minutes he said he was glad to have a rational discussion with someone and they would comply with our decision. I called "The Tech," complimented the reporter, and described the phone conversation and their willingness to comply. That was the last we heard from "Students for Struik" themselves.

"Students for Struik" came up again, however, as a topic. A meeting of our secret society, *Osiris*, was held the next week and the MIT administration wanted to hear details about the issue. Although student government had decided how they should deal with the student group, Dr. Struik was still a major campus topic. Dr. Killian and the usual group of administrators and Deans came to the meeting, joined this time by Dr. Karl Compton, Dr. Killian's predecessor as President and now Chairman of the MIT Corporation. Dr. Compton was an older, graying, almost mythically revered man on campus.

I described the Ins Comm decision at the *Osiris* meeting. I still believe, as I talked, that Dr. Compton turned to the man next to him and asked "Who is that?" True or not, I was to hear from him several days later. "Would you stop in his office to talk for a few moments?" I said "sure" and made an appointment.

Many events followed that appointment. My professional career started with it, thanks in no small part to Senator McCarthy and his well-publicized intimidations. Who else has had their career started by the accusations of Senator McCarthy and his supporters?

I was to find out first, though, that "Students for Struik" still hadn't completely disappeared. The name turned up later in a worrisome way. Because it did, the name has stayed in my mind to this day: "Should I have acted differently? Did I harm a classmate's career?" The compelling and destructive mood McCarthy had created so dominated the campus (and me), that I felt I had no choice. Civil disobedience or saying "no" to legitimate authority were not considerations. I did what was asked of me.

The reappearance of the subject began a few days after the Ins Comm meeting, as I worked in the student government offices. I got a phone call from a man with a forgettable name like Tom Williams or Dick Smith who didn't identify himself further. He asked if he could meet with me to discuss recent events on campus. I went back in my mind to the press interest in the subject and decided that must be what this is about: he wants an explanation of the conflicting headlines. I said "sure" and asked where and how would I know him. "Don't worry," he said, "I'll meet you in the lobby of your dormitory when you come back from classes tomorrow afternoon. I'll recognize you." "OK," I thought, "He's serious."

Even before I looked for him the next afternoon he came up and introduced himself. He was an ordinary-looking man in a fedora and a plain gray suit. "Could we talk for a moment in my car?" he asked. I followed him to his car, a plain gray Plymouth coupe parked around the corner from the door to the dormitory. He introduced himself again, we chatted for a moment, and he explained that he was with the CIA. Did I know what that was? I did. He said he was particularly interested in the Struik group.

"Could you provide me with the names of the students involved?" he asked.

I carried Burge Jamieson's list of names, first snatched away and then returned by the leader of the group. Five or six names were scrawled in pencil on a piece of notebook paper. I knew the name of the leader because we had talked on the phone, but I hadn't read the list. All I knew was that it was a list of names.

Without a thought I said "yes" and handed him the paper. He said "thank you," asked if I'd like a job with the CIA — he said there were lots of opportunities — and that was that. No questions about what we did, no expressed concerns, no nothing. Just names. I said "no" to the job offer; he thanked me again and left.

What about the professor at the center of all this turmoil? In addition to a list of Struik's impressive accomplishments in mathematics, "Wikipedia" (6/11) reports that Struik joined the Communist party in the Netherlands in 1919 and remained a steadfast Marxist all his life. At his 96th birthday party, quizzed as to how he stayed so active, he answered blithely that he had the "3Ms: Marriage, Mathematics and Marxism."

During the McCarthy era Struik was accused of being a Soviet spy and advocating the overthrow of government, charges he vehemently denied. Invoking the First and Fifth Amendments, he refused to answer any of 200 questions put to him during HUAC hearings. MIT suspended him from teaching, with full salary, for five years. Re-instated in 1956, he retired in 1960 as Professor Emeritus of Mathematics and died in 2000 at the age of 106.

My First Briefcase

I remember a sunny, warm afternoon when I had my meeting with Dr. Compton, Chairman of the MIT Corporation. His office was light and airy and he was in great spirits. We talked about the student group, about world affairs, and he reminisced about his time as MIT President. He was very cordial.

He told me he had a contract with the Mellon Institute of Industrial Research, an industrial research organization in Pittsburgh, and he would like some help with it. He wanted to know how the clients of the organization felt about it, and whether or not they were happy with the research programs they paid the Mellon Institute to conduct. Would I travel around the Eastern US and report to him what they said and how they felt their work was handled?

I of course said "yes" and spent the summer between my senior and graduate-student years going from company to company, talking with Presidents or Directors of Research and writing short memos to Dr. Compton about the visits. I met with him several times and with the group that had contracted with him for the study.

I also used the subject of industrial research institutes for my graduate thesis for the Master's Degree in Industrial Management at MIT. The thesis wasn't very good — I still wasn't such a good student - but I earned my Master's Degree nonetheless. And the Mellon Institute merged with the Carnegie Institute of Technology, and is now part of Carnegie-Mellon Institute of Technology.

I followed that experience with two years in the uniform of a second lieutenant in the US Army Chemical Corps. America was fighting in Korea but my time was spent in classrooms or offices in the Midwestern US. I was stationed sequentially in Illinois, Alabama, Kansas and Colorado as a kind of "Utility" second lieutenant and was plugged into administrative chores here and there. Once in Kansas while I was taking a course in Russian history at Fort Riley along with a Colonel with the Army Tank Corps, he offered me a chance to transfer to the Tank Corps. All I could think of was that I could get hurt that way. Being an administrator was just fine, thank you.

One memorable time, as I drove a back road in Kansas listening to the radio, I learned to my sad surprise that Dr. Karl Compton, Chairman of the MIT Corporation, had died. I telegraphed my condolences and was invited in return to be a pallbearer at his funeral. My father said he would pay my expenses if I wanted to go, but I couldn't because of responsibilities that week in the Army. The invitation was followed, however, by a request to return to MIT when my Army years were over, to talk with them about a job.

I went and met briefly with Dr. Killian and then with Mal Kispert, Executive Assistant to the President. Mal offered me the job of "Administrative Assistant to the President," to be concerned with office chores and specific assignments as they arose, and to be an every-day reference about student concerns.

I felt I couldn't turn down the job of working in the MIT President's office. I started in May 1955 and was appointed to various internal management groups. A common extra job was to help visitors to the MIT campus get settled. I met and had a pleasant talk with the physicist Neils Bohr and helped publicize his talks to an assembled MIT student body. I met the British Ambassador to the US and one or two other dignitaries when they came to campus.

I drew up an organizational chart of the MIT administration which looked like nothing more than a confusing mass of lines and little boxes. (MIT was like that.) I was still a member of *Osiris* and attended its meetings. I researched and wrote a paper on the history of football as a student sport at MIT.

As I gained experience and familiarity, I made friends with others, including Jeff Wylie, the Public Relations Director, who was later to be important to my work in the White House. I was asked to tell the "Dean of Student Aid," another friend, that higher-ups wanted him to spend more money on scholarships and loans. He did, of course, and as time went by I was given other messages to carry to other people. The only rejection I remember was that I couldn't find a faculty member whom I believe didn't want to be found. I suspect that he did not want to be told something by the President's office.

A friend called my job that of the "Vice-President of Minutiae" but through it, and after five years as a student, I was familiar with the workings of the Institute. I was awed by the faculty's apparent superior stature. As they say, all people are equals but some are more equal than others. Some of the faculty seemed to expect frequent compliments and recognition of their superior role. I treated them with great respect, however they acted.

One of the committees I served on was searching for a new faculty member: "Is he the best in his field in the world?" was a question asked about one candidate after another.

At times I felt I was just a naïve and ambitious country kid trying to find himself and his life work. I had majored in Industrial Management but working as an Assistant to the President at MIT was hardly industrial management. MIT, I decided after a while, wasn't my life work. It was an interesting job but I was ready to move on. Ambition and restlessness played major roles in my decision. I guess they always have.

My restlessness coincided with the Russian launch of the satellite "Sputnik." President Eisenhower, in response to the stunning Russian accomplishment, spoke on national television. Dr. Killian invited the Executive Assistant to the President — my immediate boss — and me to his house to watch and hear the President's speech.

President Eisenhower said he was appointing Dr. Killian, President of MIT, to be his Science Advisor. We watched TV in awe as a big event for the country and of course for MIT unfolded. The MIT community seemed pleased that one of their own was going to straighten out whatever problems the country had. Newspapers described him as the country's "Missile Czar," and were very supportive.

One day shortly later, when Dr. Killian was back in Cambridge, I asked for a moment with him and asked if he had any suggestions for me and a new job. He did, and asked if I would like to assist him in his work in the White House. I was astounded; I had no idea he planned to take an assistant. He said my job would be as staff assistant to the President's Science Advisory Committee, the "PSAC" and its panel on Education, to handle press relations for the Science Advisor's office should any be needed, and generally to help him however I could.

I, of course, said "yes" and moved with my wife and young son to Washington.

A Year at the White House
1958

Our Digs

The government gave the newly-appointed President's Science Adviser a spacious suite of offices in the pile of gray stone next to the White House now named the "Eisenhower Executive Office Building." The building had once been the offices of "State, War and Navy." That once all three of those departments could be housed in one building, but now have enormous complexes of their own, comments on the growth of government.

The Executive Office Building (Wikipedia photo). Our offices were on the second floor on the other side, facing the White House.

I learned from the beginning how much of the federal government had little to do with the President and vice versa. Acquaintances I made in Washington talked of "The President" as a separate entity and would imply that they worked for the building operators or some other federal entity, not for "The President," whoever he might be at the moment.

Tens of thousands of employees go about routine daily tasks without any White House supervision and without publicity, while the President and his personal staff go about theirs. The White House and the rest of the federal government seemed to me to be almost distinct entities. I felt we had been brought to Washington by important and direct Presidential action; some seemed to see our arrival as just another ho-hum group moving in.

Among our offices was an interesting conference room with false interior walls. Security officials would walk with their sensing devices between the outer and inner walls of this conference room periodically, testing for electronic intruders or "bugs." Our offices, however, were not as closely guarded as one might expect; coming to work in the morning involved simply showing identification. No sensing devices, no challenges of any sort; just walk through. To get into the White House proper, however, we crossed a short alley between the two buildings and passed additional security.

I was involved twice in use of that conference room. Once a dozen Congressmen asked for audience with Dr. Killian to press their case for some issue. (It seemed to me a measure of relative status when it took twelve Representatives to gain audience with one White House appointee.) The second time Navy officials wanted Dr. Killian's scientists to see a film showing a problem with the fins of a Poseidon missile as it launched underwater from a submarine.

My primary responsibility was to serve as technical assistant to an Advisory Council sub-committee on education. The group, with Dr. Lee DuBridge, President of California Institute of Technology as chairman, met two or three times. They discussed the current state of scientific and technical education vigorously, and then turned their deliberations over to Dr. John Burchard, Dean of Humanities at MIT, friend, good writer and a professional fully conversant with issues in technical education. He wrote a paper which became a booklet entitled "Education for the Age of Science." I edited the report and saw that it was printed in thousands of copies and distributed to some 16,000 high schools all across America.

The report led to some additional effort to improve high school science education but was largely forgotten. MIT and other college physics faculty, with Dr. Edwin H. Land of Polaroid Corporation and a staff member housed with him as participants, designed a new curriculum for high school physics. My impression is that it was a rigorous curriculum that wasn't widely adopted.

I feel the sub-committee made one serious mistake which consigned the report to join so many others, stacked on a virtual bookshelf and largely ignored. The group felt that the cost of the changes they recommended should be included, so they estimated a $3 billion price tag without specifying where such a sum would come from.

Because the report was dense and dealt with an unfamiliar topic, the $3 billion figure was the easiest fact for many journalists and observers to find. "$3 billion for education" became a common headline. The President, I believe, wanted no part of recommending such a sum. I don't believe the report ever got much support from the White House or education offices in government.

Meetings, Travels and Disappointments

I was involved in one noteworthy event regarding the report. It became a major topic of a morning Cabinet meeting with the President. The government officials involved with education and/or technology were present, including Vice President Nixon, the head of the National Science Foundation, various cabinet officials, and the President himself.

The meeting was held in the Cabinet room of the White House. A large oblong table had chairs aligned neatly around it, with chairs with 6-inch taller backs in the middle of each long side for the President and Vice-President. The white bookshelves of the beautiful room held few objects, most notably a memorable small bust of Abraham Lincoln. Chairs for other officials not seated at the table filled out the room.

Once the crowd was assembled, we settled in for a brief wait. Suddenly a staff person entered and called out "Ladies and Gentlemen, the President of the United States." We stood, President Eisenhower entered, said "sit down, sit down," and the meeting was underway.

The Secretary of State John Foster Dulles, was on his deathbed and was clearly on the President's mind. The President said sadly that he had wanted to give "Foster" some awards he felt he deserved. He called Mrs. Dulles and asked if he could visit him in the hospital. Mrs. Dulles replied that she really didn't think that would be a good idea, that he would be too affected, and that she would give the awards to him.

The President followed that comment by saying he knew the meeting today was about education and wanted to describe an event that dealt with the subject. A few months before, he had met with a lady who had been identified as the outstanding teacher of the year. He said they had a pleasant visit and conversation. She wrote a nice thank you note and he replied at some length to follow on with the conversation. With disappointment in his voice, he noted that she never wrote back.

With those two anecdotes from the President, the meeting proceeded. Dr. Killian introduced Dr. DuBridge, who summarized the report. I stood at the end of the table and flipped the pages of a 30" x 40" pad of paper on which were printed the major points of the report, though not including the $3 billion figure. Little or no discussion followed, and Dr. Killian, Dr. DuBridge and I were excused.

I sensed that Vice President Nixon looked at me closely as I flipped pages, briefly, as if to size me up. His dark visage and intense look still stand out in my mind. I had a friend who refused a position on Nixon's staff because he believed the Vice President demanded complete devotion, extensive hard work and long hours from his subordinates. My friend wasn't interested in such demands.

Dr. Killian and I went to Cape Canaveral to assess the status and cost of our newest, heavy-duty missile intended for military purposes, and to look in on the effort to launch a "Vanguard" satellite. The civilian Vanguard group was preparing to launch a grapefruit-sized, radio-transmitting satellite. Our military missile launch pad and the civilian Vanguard site were two very different scenes.

The enthusiastic group preparing the Vanguard rocket all wore uniforms, I believe, and caps with a logo emblazoned on them. With their boyish enthusiasm they seemed to me to be a group of space exploration boy scouts. The military effort was more professional and well directed, with senior military involved and notably more sober demeanor.

The Vanguard group launched their first rocket in December 1957. It failed dramatically, tipping over and spilling its small satellite onto the launch pad. I can't imagine a failure with more Freudian implications of impotence. The failure, fully televised and spectacular, must have convinced many Americans that we were even further behind the Soviets in this new and unfamiliar world of space exploration.

A common question troubled many at the time. Werner von Braun, who had worked for years on the Nazi rocket program, and many of his staff were picked up near the end of War II and employed by the Army to develop American missilery. Van Braun boasted that he could launch a full-sized, professional rocket and satellite with only the "go-ahead" and a little work. He could reverse the embarrassing Vanguard failure.

The President never gave that "go-ahead" because I understood he didn't want the Army to control America's efforts in space. (I've since been told that another reason influenced him: he didn't want to stimulate an expensive new competition with the Soviets.) He assigned our efforts in space to a civilian agency, now named the National Aeronautics and Space Administration, NASA.

We also traveled to Sandia National Laboratories in New Mexico for a visit and, I believe, to convince the group that the Science Advisor, and by implication the President, were interested in and supportive of their work.

Two incidental events stand out from this visit. We flew in a White House plane which I didn't realize until then carried a full-sized bed for its principal occupant, to help make a long flight more comfortable. I had a chair such as those in an airline's first-class section.

Secondly, when we returned to Washington in the wee hours of the morning, someone (I suspect a reporter looking for a story) apparently recognized the standard car of the White House fleet, a black four-door Mercury sedan, and followed us closely for some distance, repeatedly trying to see who was in the car. I suspect he was hoping to see some nubile young woman climb out, leaving behind a graying and recognizable Washington dignitary. All he got was me. I'm sure he was disappointed.

Radar Contact With Venus

An MIT friend accounted for an interesting event during my Washington year. Jeff Wylie, the MIT Public Relations Director, called me one afternoon. Dr. Killian was away and unreachable. Jeff was at a conference at the Lincoln Laboratories, a laboratory near Boston affiliated with MIT and site of important research in radar.

He called me to report that the laboratory had made radar contact with the planet Venus. This was an important and impressive event, especially in these times of concern about space exploration. Jeff thought the President might be interested in recognizing the accomplishment. I noted what he told me, wrote a short memo, asked Dr. Killian's secretary to type it up and walked it across the alley to the office of Pierre Salinger, then the colorful press secretary to the President.

There was a glitch in the story. It had taken a year to sort out the contact with Venus from background noise. I don't know if this was a real problem or simply that the group hadn't rushed to sort out the information. Anyway, after a few minutes, Salinger called me, I suspect, to see if I was a real person and to ask me, "What's all this about a year to check out the radar contact?" I told him "It's the straight story." Salinger said "OK" and hung up.

The accomplishment was being described to several hundred people, I heard later, when a secretary rushed in to whisper to the speaker, "There's a telegram from the White House coming in!" A telegram from President Eisenhower arrived, congratulating the group. The speaker read it aloud to great applause. The next day the contact with Venus was reported on the front page of the New York Times.

I remember another event in my role as a secondary PR official. An investigative reporter from TIME Magazine contacted me and proved his nature as a gregarious but pushy and aggressive man. He wanted comments about the Advisory Committee's work from some member. One of the members, the famous physicist I. I. Rabi, spoke to him at some length on condition of anonymity. The reporter quoted Rabi without identifying him, just saying that a member of the Committee had commented about its work.

Accompanying the story in TIME was a photograph of Rabi, identified as "a member of the President's Science Advisory Committee." What the article didn't ask was "Do you want to know who told us all this? Can you take a hint?"

Another task arose when Dr. Killian told me that the President wanted to see a "transistor," a new device very much in technical and commercial headlines at the time. It fell to me to find one so the next lunchtime I went to an electronics store to buy a transistor, just a transistor. The clerk looked at me quizzically but found one. I bought it and gave it to Dr. Killian. Presumably it found its way to Eisenhower's desk.

Though I watched a Presidential press conference once or twice, I had contact with Eisenhower only one more time, at a Christmas gathering in the East Room. He invited all his staff, supposedly, and wandered around with his bodyguards, carefully shaking hands and wishing everyone "Merry Christmas." He seemed to me to be a tired old man.

He gave each of us a print of one of his paintings as a Christmas present. (He was a better President than painter but I framed it and still treasure the painting.) Reportedly 600 copies were printed so that may be a measure of the size of his staff at the time. I doubt, however, that as many as two hundred people gathered for the event.

Dr. Killian's role at the White House diminished in importance as time went by. He had been warned that he had credibility at the beginning but as public attention drifted away he would steadily lose influence. Meanwhile, he was being pressed to return to MIT where his interim replacement was in a compromised position, not being President but facing issues that needed a President to resolve. So after about eighteen months Dr. Killian resigned, to far less publicity than he had received when he took the job, and returned to MIT.

Though I was asked to stay by Dr. Killian's successor, I resolved to leave at the same time. Polaroid and Cambridge became my next stop.

Polaroid: Behind Blue Doors

1957

Back to Cambridge

The 4 ½ years I worked for Polaroid Corporation in Cambridge, Mass., and around Edwin H. Land, "authentic genius" and the creator of the Company, were the most influential of my life.

My informal reminiscence of the period is drawn from my notes at the time, my memories and a review of some current literature about Land and Polaroid. I'll discuss the man, the Company, some of the people who worked around him, the mood he created and some of the methods of his work. Finally I'll describe the conditions that led me to quit the Company.

In many ways it was a wild ride.

Before Dr. Land died in 1991 he asked an assistant to destroy all his personal records and notes. If that assistant was the presidential secretary I knew, Natalie Fuld, and it well may have been, she would do a good job of it. The work is said to have taken three years. Three weeks or perhaps three months make sense, but three years?

His secretary may have been with him from the late fifties, when I was there, to the time he retired. She seemed at the time to be about my age, so when Land died she would have been in her early sixties. A reasonable corporate act would be to invite her to fulfill Land's wishes, take all the time she needed to destroy his records, and retire in three years at sixty-five. That would be a fitting tribute to her lifetime of loyalty.

I've been asked what secrets were so monumental that all record of them had to be destroyed. I think they had little or nothing to do with the popular first guess, evidence of female anger at a relationship gone wrong. To my mind there is a more believable explanation.

Land was a very private man. Only once or twice did I hear him mention his private life, and the privacy of his mailroom supports this theory. Some confidential documents were kept there, possibly including national secrets regarding his Washington life, Company secrets, the technical contributions of other people, and personal records. They were things he wanted no one but himself and his secretary to see. She saw to it that no one was admitted to that room.

I think he wanted his legacy as a genius to survive as he had built it. He cultured his public image carefully. Free access by others to his private records would have an unknown and possibly negative effect on that image. Better just to destroy all those records and thus his personal life and public image would be as protected as was possible for him.

Natalie, the secretary I knew, was discrete, loyal and devoted. She seemed content with the title "Secretary." Others with less contact with Land assumed the title "Assistant to the President" largely on their own initiative since Land usually didn't assign titles to anyone. Two or three of those who I feel could correctly be called such will be identified as I go along. Natalie was one and certainly deserved such a title had she wanted it.

I don't know of anyone, however, who has written an intimate portrait of the man at that extraordinary time, the early nineteen sixties. The Polaroid camera and film became a beacon to the success of American technology; the speed and ease of use of the product increased; color film was introduced; the Company and its stock price grew dramatically. The public saw Land as a kind of folk hero. The period deserves portrayal.

I write a summary of my experiences and hope it will be useful to understanding the man, his methods and his associates. I admired Land greatly and enjoyed my work at Polaroid. This essay is meant to be a tribute to him.

My Story

My story starts in October, 1957.

The country was in an uproar. The Russians had launched "Sputnik," the world's first man-made satellite, into orbit over a completely unprepared American public. We watched it sail far overhead from our own streets and backyards. The event was alarming.

The Russians were more technologically adept than we knew. Questions flew: "Are we in danger?" "Are we behind the Russians in missiles?" "I can see their satellite; can they see me or even shoot at me?" "What is a satellite anyway, and how does it work?" "Could we launch a satellite?" We were stunned and confused.

Dr. Killian took a leave of absence from MIT to take the job as Science Advisor in Washington. He asked a number of eminent scientists and engineers to join him in a President's Science Advisory Committee to advise the President and periodically to meet with Eisenhower personally. Many of the people he chose were already involved in relevant technical efforts. Others were executives of companies doing important work for the military. Their job was to help us be sure the nation's efforts in science and technology were headed in the right direction and to identify problems and shortcomings.

Dr. Killian asked Edwin H. Land, the widely proclaimed model of American success in technology, to join the committee. Land carried three titles at Polaroid: Chairman of the Board, President and Director of Research, and was the Company's largest stockholder as well. When he listed his three titles, invariably he would identify "Director of Research" as the most important.

Land's stature, his expertise in optics and photography, his experience with government and his skill with words made him a logical and valued member of the committee.

Land and his Company were well known, but this was the first time I met him. His reputation at the time, as I recall, was at once stellar as an entrepreneur and modestly downplayed by academics as a huckster. Some considered him to be a kind of winning and articulate "Wizard of Oz," whose technology wouldn't meet rigorous academic standards. When I heard subtly expressed criticism of him now and then, I figured that it came either from not knowing him, characteristic academic downplaying of successful industrial entrepreneurship, or from jealousy, or perhaps from all three.

After he held the job in Washington for about eighteen months, Dr. Killian chose to leave his position and I decided to leave as well. I was invited to return to work at MIT or to stay in the Washington office with his replacement but I wasn't keen on either option, so I asked Land if he needed a "research administrator" at Polaroid.

I had decided that administering industrial research and helping researchers would be an appropriate use of my skills and education. Polaroid seemed to be an almost luminous place to pursue such a career and, what's more, now I knew the man who had made it happen.

"Come to Cambridge to meet with me and my staff," Land said. I went, and in the summer of 1959 started work as a bright eyed, 29 year old, self-titled "research administrator" of Polaroid's "innovative laboratories."

**Edwin H. Land, from an article in "Fortune" magazine,
April 1959, entitled "The Magic That Made Polaroid."**

The Company

The popular story was that one Christmas holiday Land took photos with his daughter. She asked him why they had to wait to see the result. He wondered the same thing, saw how to do it, and set out to produce instant photography.

Polaroid Corporation introduced the first cameras to provide finished photos instantly at Jordan Marsh in Boston in November, 1948. The few dozen cameras available sold out almost immediately.

Demand skyrocketed from those first few cameras. By 1950 more than 4000 hurriedly contracted dealers sold Polaroid cameras; by 1963 five million cameras had been sold. Many people clearly felt they needed an alternative to the common, familiar but time-consuming Kodak photo process. It took so much time to develop a photo that it left the excitement of the "photo moment" well behind. The Polaroid camera with its instantly developing film met that need.

"Fortune" magazine, April 1950, in an article entitled "The Magic That Made Polaroid," introduced its article with these grand words:

> "The sixty-second Land camera has made Polaroid a daz-
> zling growth company. How Polaroid grew from nowhere to
> second place in its industry is the story of an authentic genius
> turned loose in industry."

Thomas Alva Edison defined genius as "1 percent inspiration and 99 percent perspiration." If Land's response to his daughter's question qualifies as "inspiration," he clearly added "perspiration." He and others worked vigorously and at great lengths to realize the dream. Land qualifies as a genius.

When I joined the Company in 1959, the Company's annual sales were about $90 million and it employed about 2500 people. Its principal offices were in Cambridge and its manufacturing in Waltham, Mass., with other facilities and warehouses around Cambridge and elsewhere in the country. Its sales and manufacturing operations, though I didn't know them well, were run competently.

The Man

A detailed biography of Dr. Land is beyond my reach, but many things about him should be noted. Among them:

He never earned a bachelor's degree, but many colleges granted him honorary degrees. He became wealthy as the founding President of a successful company whose stock was renowned and widely coveted. He and his family owned some 750,000 shares of the Company stock.

He was an important contributor to the nation's defense efforts during World War II. He made important contributions to the design of the U2 spy plane used for aerial surveillance during the Cold War. He became an adviser to President Eisenhower and the President gave Nikita Khrushchev a Polaroid camera as an example of American ingenuity. In 1963 Land was awarded the highest civilian honor, the Presidential Medal of Freedom, for his work in aerial reconnaissance.

Polarizing filters, which he introduced and were the first business of the Company, have a great many important military, photographic and other uses.

As a color theorist he published a captivating theory in "Scientific American" about his research in color vision which seemed to turn that esoteric world upside down.

Land's experience and his personal attributes were surrounded by an aura of success and importance. He was in his early 50's, a spellbinding and charismatic talker, and good looking in an intense, dark way. He had created a famous Company, owned three quarters of a million shares of its stock that gained perhaps a million dollars one day and lost a few hundred thousand the next as the stock worked its way upward. Wherever he went the successes of the Company and his reputation preceded him, and the dollar signs reinforced the impression. His very presence seemed to be an exciting adventure.

Land's public mannerisms often seemed almost shy and retiring. When he spoke publicly his words came in halting, irregular phrases as if he was checking to see if you approved, or as if he were thinking up the words as he went along. His speaking seemed to demand that you listen, even perhaps to help him say what he was saying. His way of talking, his often provocative comments and of course his public stature insured that you listened.

Once, when Dr. Killian asked Land to repeat to President Eisenhower a short and stirring speech he had given in a meeting preparing for a visit with the President, his response was "What did I say?" Reportedly, he, repeated his words effectively.

A measure of the articulate and inspiring message Land could deliver was given at his "Arthur D. Little" lecture in May, 1957. He had spent two weeks meeting with students and faculty in small groups and then spoke to a large audience in an MIT auditorium. These first few paragraphs of the speech and the sentiments behind them, made appropriate to the audience or person he was speaking to at the time, were hallmarks of his personality. They lay beneath everyday conversation with him; it's easy to understand why working with him was such an exciting experience. This was a wonderful speech.

"The Age of Greatness"

"What do I mean by greatness as I have used it in the title of this lecture? What do I mean by the Generation of Greatness?" I mean that in this age, in this country, there is an opportunity for the development of man's intellectual, cultural, and spiritual potentialities that has never existed before in the history of our species. I mean not simply an opportunity for greatness for a few, but an opportunity for greatness for the many.

"I believe that each young person is different from any other who has ever lived, as different as his fingerprints: that he could bring to the world a wonderful and special way of solving unsolved problems, that in his special way, he can be great. Now don't misunderstand me. I recognize that this merely great person, as distinguished from the genius, will not be able to bridge from field to field. He will not have the ideas that shorten the solution of problems by hundreds of years. He will not suddenly say that mass is energy, that is genius. But within his own field he will make things grow and flourish; he will grow happy doing it. Helping other people in his field, and to that field he will add things that would not have been added, had he not come along.

"I believe there are two opposing theories of history, and you have to make your choice. Either you believe that this kind of individual greatness does exist and can be nurtured and developed, that such great individuals can be part of a cooperative community while they continue to be their happy, flourishing, contributing selves -- or else you believe that there is some mystical, cyclical, overriding, predetermined, cultural law -- a historic determinism.

"The great contribution of science is to say that this second theory is nonsense. The great contribution of science is to demonstrate that a person can regard the world as chaos, but can find in himself a method of perceiving, within that chaos, small arrangements of order, that out of himself, and out of the order that previous scientists have generated, he can make things that are exciting and thrilling to make, that are deeply spiritual contributions to himself and to his friends. The scientist comes to the world and says, "I do not understand the divine source, but I know, in a way that I don't understand, that out of chaos I can make order, out of loneliness I can make friendship, out of ugliness I can make beauty.

"I believe that men are born this way -- that all I know that each of the undergraduates with whom I talked shares this belief. Each of these men felt secretly -- it was his very special secret and his deepest secret -- that he could be great."

His Space

Polaroid's office buildings were located on Osborne Street in Cambridge and nearby. Land delighted in telling visitors that the Company lay between Harvard and MIT, thus implying something important about the Company.

Land's own building was a large, three-story former furniture factory with its own historic place in science. One outside brick wall carried a plaque that identified it as the building in which Alexander Graham Bell uttered the famous words "Mr. Watson, come here," over the first working telephone. Knowing Land's penchant for self-promotion, I suspect that plaque and its nod to genius influenced his purchase of the building.

Another building, across Osborne Street, housed additional corporate offices and a chemical laboratory. A research vice-president led this research. Other Company facilities, including marketing and manufacturing and their respective vice-presidents, were elsewhere in the area.

Blue outside doors on Land's building opened from the street into a mysterious dark corridor, past the door to the President's office suite, to a door opening into the "innovative" laboratories. Here lay both Land and his magic laboratories. To enter the building through the blue doors and into its dark corridor was to enter a domain of mystery and adventure.

Land liked to say that Polaroid operated at the "interface of science and art," and this dark corridor contained a quiet example. The dark corridor displayed a number of beautiful Polaroid photos hung at eye level along one long wall. Spotlights mounted inconspicuously on the ceiling lit each photo separately. The entry into his building thus became a mystical art gallery displaying examples of the successful use of ordinary Polaroid film.

Land commented frequently on visual phenomena, and a different display of photographs once gave him an opportunity to show several of us how the location of the spotlights affected the images. He demonstrated that the images could appear flat or suddenly quite vivid simply by moving the spotlights back and forth along the ceiling. The angle of the light illuminating the photographs made a big difference.

Land's building included his five-room office suite and the "black and white lab," the "red and white lab," where Land explored a color phenomenon different from the color film work conducted upstairs in the second floor "color lab," and a particularly secret "emulsions laboratory." A staff of engineers reporting to an engineering vice-president and empty space filled the rest of the building.

Land's suite of offices contained his own office, a reception area with desks for two secretaries, two small offices for assistants and a large and very private mailroom with plain tables spread neatly with letters, papers and reports. His personal office had two heavy soundproofing doors, one opening to the reception area and the other to the black and white laboratories.

The heavy soundproofing doors helped make certain that no conversations, or any evidence that Land was there at all, could escape his office. I never once heard Land raise his voice so it seems unlikely that he was trying to muffle his own words. My unproven intuition was that the doors were installed when the loud voice of someone, an angry woman perhaps, spilled out into his reception room. Whatever prompted their installation happened before my time and before the secure line to Washington was installed.

Land's office was lined with bookshelves and hundreds of books on photography and other subjects, with here and there a copy of a primer on photography he could give away if an important visitor asked about the technology. His desk was often enlivened by photographs from his latest camera, a mock-up of the camera itself, a dozen or so pipes, and perhaps a stack of the "most pressing" mail he needed to answer. His desk also held a number of telephones, including one or two directly connected to a colleague or employee, and a secure telephone, with its voice-scrambling hardware locked in the basement, that connected him to Washington.

A dozen or so spectacular 30" x 40" photographs by the master photographer Ansel Adams rested against the bookshelves, often leaning casually against one another. The photographs were beautiful: of Yosemite, of a moon rising over a southwestern town, of a horse sunlit in a distant landscape. These museum-quality and valuable photos emphasized the Company's role in art.

Land treated the two heavy doors differently from one another. I felt he treated the one to his reception room as if it led to the Corporation and to his role as President and Chairman of the Board. Visitors, corporate vice-presidents or others with business to conduct would sit there patiently until Land came out or his secretary sent them in.

He seemed to treat his loyal secretary, Natalie Fuld, whose desk was just outside this door, as his conscience and visible reminder of his corporate responsibilities. He would come out periodically to discuss his appointments and obligations with her. She would screen his calls and answer cautiously as to his availability.

Natalie jealously guarded the private mailroom in his suite as her own private domain. Periodically she would walk with him past the tables and their papers in that room, taking notes and dictation item by item. I saw the inside of the room only once or twice and then just from the doorway.

The other soundproofing door to his office opened into the black and white laboratories and seemed the more favored of the two. Meroe Morse, his amanuensis and originally my boss, had her office just outside that door. She could talk with him almost at will as he left his office for laboratory work. Her ability to contact Land was casual and respectful. Meroe was important to the Company because of her substantial talents and experience, but also because she had easy access to Land.

Land delighted in saying that he had the title and role as Director of Research, along with his other titles, because research was too important to delegate. He did seem more willing to delegate corporate responsibilities to others than to skip occasional personal contact with researchers. The two doors to his office, one to his Presidential duties and the other to his research, seemed to help him keep the roles separate.

The People

Worn wooden floors, white walls and plain laboratory tables furnished the black and white laboratories inexpensively. Researchers, equipment and materials spread through four or five large rooms in these labs, with here and there a sizeable darkroom. Land's own red and white research, the subject of a "Scientific American" article that caused much excitement, filled one of the large rooms.

The color film laboratory, working on the color version of instant developing film and managed by Howie Rogers was upstairs, and an emulsions laboratory occupied space entered through its own outside door. An applied physics laboratory, managed first by David Gray until he left the Company, was located in another building.

My responsibilities as an administrator involved the film labs. My office was a walled, widened space in the black and white labs. I never saw the emulsion nor the physics labs, nor asked about them. I learned quickly that privacy was an important value at Polaroid and discretion was always appropriate. I didn't need to know what the other labs did, very little information was volunteered, and I didn't ask.

Land, as Director of Research, oversaw the black and white and color film laboratories, his own red and white research laboratory, the emulsion and applied physics laboratories. This was essentially his research empire. Other research, including research into new chemicals for color film, was conducted across the street and delegated to its own Vice-President.

Roughly fifty people worked in his laboratories. As I recall, only one researcher had a doctorate; the rest did not. Land was democratic; he treated everyone in the labs respectfully, regardless of academic standing. Titles to differentiate one employee from another were a nuisance in his research environment. He relied on some people more heavily than on others, of course, but even that changed sporadically. Authority and position were attributes a person seemed to have or not have, based on longevity with Polaroid, the importance of the job and fundamentally with closeness to Land.

Jobs were spread among four or five sets of overlapping responsibilities. Lab directors, individual researchers — often young women — supervisors, technicians and photographers filled the rooms. An individual might find his or her job change from one of these jobs to another almost overnight. Researchers might one day be asked to take scenic photos and a supervisor to run tests acting as a technician. Almost anyone could be asked to test a potential new product.

`My role, too, could change from budgets and personnel work to another responsibility. When his lawyers discovered Land test-driving a Chevrolet Corvette, a real muscle car, no doubt thinking of his liability, they wouldn't let him drive it back to the dealer. I drove it back.

Another time he asked me to find a comfortable house nearby that could be used as a relaxing retreat for meetings of the Company's "Operating Policy Committee." Funeral homes were the only such houses I could find in Cambridge that fit his criteria. Land agreed with me when I reported the results of my search. I suspect he had looked himself.

Earlier in corporate history, Land spoke of a "sun-and-satellite" system of operation, where one person would be given a responsibility and others would gather round and work as "satellites" to him or her, their "sun." The sun-and-satellite system sounded great and did seem occasionally to be an organizing principle. It could be used to explain how jobs and roles changed frequently.

**Land, in a photo I took, using the two-syringe device
to mix development chemicals.**

Land's own role had great influence on the "sun's" authority. Researchers knew it and wanted to work with him. It was a comedown to be guided by Meroe or some other supervisor after starting with Land, but if a project migrated to another supervisor, researchers were told that Land's extensive responsibilities wouldn't allow him to work long with just one person or project. A replacement supervisor would become a substitute.

The heads of the laboratories, Meroe Morse, working in black and white film, Howie Rogers, working in color film, Nigel Daw, in Land's own explorations of color who worked without assistants, and others in the optics and emulsion labs were his principal research supervisors. They didn't experience a frequent kaleidoscopic range of responsibilities but even they could occasionally pick up a new task.

MEROE MORSE

Meroe, daughter of the Princeton mathematician Marston Morse, was beautiful, in her late 30's and a graduate of Smith College. She had studied both as a concert harpist and as an artist. She brought an artistic temperament and substantial organizing skills to her job as laboratory director. She became thoroughly imbued with Land's methods, seemed to understand him and was devoted to him. She was careful never to claim that she represented him unless she had a specific quote to recite. When she spoke, however, her words were often respected as if they had come from Land himself.

As an artist Meroe had entertained audiences by completing a picture from a single line that someone, a child perhaps, drew on a large sheet of paper. She told me her first assignment at Polaroid was to draw the same picture on white paper with black ink and then on black paper with white ink. Land told her he was uncertain which way to proceed in photography and wanted to see the effectiveness of such different renditions.

Meroe had an important role that she said Land never defined. Though she didn't have the formal title, she would certainly be considered his assistant. She distributed the testing he wanted or she felt was necessary among technicians or their supervisors, and evaluated, organized and presented the results. She helped maintain the secrecy of the work and was publicly very close-mouthed about it. She helped create a crisis atmosphere when necessary or desirable. She helped keep peace among arguing researchers if the need arose. Occasionally she would organize a group admittance to Land's office, usually to discuss a research topic. She was very much the leader of the black and white laboratory; only when Land himself was present would her role become less supervisory and more subservient.

Meroe spent most of her days in the laboratory but occasionally entered into corporate meetings if Land invited her. She had worked with and around many of these people for years and fit in with both familiarity and reserve. I felt that her attitudes about people and issues influenced Land substantially and might well be discussed with him after a meeting she attended. Participants knew she had his ear and treated her with cordial and careful respect.

In addition to the leadership roles, Meroe had the normal administrative duties of any research manager. Budgets, personnel management, equipment and space usage all needed her attention, but she wasn't very interested. Land was willing to hire a research administrator because Meroe wanted help with that work. Her disinterest led to my job.

Working for and with Meroe was a pleasure. She was respectful and specific in describing her needs. Her first comments to me proved quite true: "I always ask questions first and shoot second," she said, "quite differently than the military." Normally she was easy to work for and accessible. When it was called for, however, she could be completely authoritative and decisive. She was always pleased to turn over to me a task she didn't relish and seemed grateful that I was there to take it. We worked well together.

HOWARD ROGERS

The director of the instant color film laboratory, Howie Rogers, had a somewhat less immediate working relationship with Land than did Meroe. He had been with Land since 1936 and was a close personal friend. Howie's color laboratory was many feet away and a story above Land's offices. He seldom let a day go by, however, without an early evening visit or a telephone conversation.

**Meroe Morse and Howie Rogers in a photo posed for
the same issue of "Fortune" magazine.**

Land had once, in the early days of the camera, listed a number of uncompleted film projects on a blackboard with the word "color" in a lower corner. Howie said he'd like to work on that, and the project started with him working half-time on instant color film. The work doubled in scope nearly every year and picked up massive assistance in the 1950's from the chemical laboratories across Osborne Street which researched and provided color-producing chemicals for use in film.

Polaroid suffered reverses during the fifteen-year gestation of color film but the project was maintained. The steady support Land gave the color work is a tribute to his perseverance and to his loyalty to an employee who returned it. Howie devoted many years of his life to instant color film.

THE YOUNG WOMEN

Perhaps a dozen mostly young women had individual responsibilities, doing routine work themselves or aided now and then by a technician. Often they were women with recent college degrees and quick and inquiring minds, but none of them I recall had an advanced degree. Land said that such minds were more important than minds trained specifically in science or technology. The subject of their college studies was not an issue, but a Smith College graduate seemed to be the ideal.

Land talked with me once at some length because one senior and valued employee, David Gray, Director of the Applied Physics laboratory, had submitted his resignation. Gray told Land he felt incomplete because he didn't have a Doctor's degree, and that he got no stimulation from his associates at Polaroid. Land was visibly upset; Gray had an important role in the research, particularly in camera optics. This using of a doctor's degree as a status symbol, Land said, seems to be "some holdover from English aristocracy." He said he just didn't understand.

Land cited Lucretia, one of the young women researchers without an advanced degree. "At Polaroid we are perfectly content," he said, "to associate events in nature with one another to our own liking, and nothing in nature says this is impossible. Nature doesn't care how our projects come out. We're free to work on them in any way that seems promising. This is fine," he said, "so long as the association of events remains true and useful. Advanced degrees have nothing to do with it. Lucretia does this," Land said, "because she is not trying to compete with others in stature or in any other way. She is content simply to be useful."

The young women often started work with an interesting project, use of a camera and unlimited film. One was charged with trying to define beauty in color as distinct from beauty in black and white. Where did color add to, and where did it detract from, the beauty of a scene? Another had the job of placing the human face in its most pleasing shade of gray. Film could be made to respond widely to variations in the illumination of a scene. If a face were properly exposed, where should the face fit in grayness in the image and how rapidly should other light levels climb or fall away from the face?

Other women were working on new film types or film for new cameras, or on more immediate projects such as increasing film speed or its quality for professional use. Others worked on mechanical devices, new ways to spread developing fluid on a sheet of coated paper, or new ways to handle and measure the "ideal" length of a photograph.

Not all of the projects were film research related: One snowy December afternoon, Land decided he wanted a new car with four-wheel drive so he could navigate through snowy streets. He asked one young woman to buy him a new car by quitting time. She went to a dealer and returned with a full description of the car and its cost. Land sent her back to buy it. The dealer couldn't get it ready in time, however, so the purchase had to wait. I suspect Land was impatient with her; he wanted a new car immediately and cost was not an issue.

These women seemed to epitomize the laboratory to others in the Company. To them it must have seemed to be full of bright and beautiful young women. Their presence often brought a leer from commentators. I was teased that I was hired to run a harem.

SUPERVISORS, TECHNICIANS AND OTHERS

The job of the technicians was to run through the experiments, to mix the chemicals, to make and measure the numerable variations in the process. Supervisors organized the work of one or several technicians to be sure the work was orderly and thorough. Researchers were praised for insights which fit into the goals of their project, but insight was not generally expected. There were plenty of new ideas.

Land liked to lead by demonstration and by success, and almost never said "no" to a specific request. His usual method was simply not to answer whenever he couldn't acquiesce. Even with many technicians available, ideas burst forth which couldn't be tried for lack of time or people or because they didn't seem promising. Weaker new ideas simply didn't get effort applied to them.

A few other, more senior researchers had spent some years with Land and held research roles without management responsibilities. This group included one or two mature women. My secretary and Meroe's were the only secretaries in the labs. All were were paid satisfactory wages and had jobs to do; inventing was not necessarily one of them.

ANSEL ADAMS AND OTHER PHOTOGRAPHERS

Ansel Adams had a contract with Polaroid first established in 1948. He and Land admired each other greatly. Ansel described his first extended contact with Land in glowing terms in his autobiography. The contract called for him to come East about two weeks a year, often with an assistant, to work with Polaroid.

Land said he told Ansel (we all called him Ansel) the reason photography was considered a minor art form was that all too often it appeared in minor form, in a snapshot or small photo. He felt Ansel should work on larger images. Scaled up to 30" x 40," Adams' images could be truly spectacular, and hardly minor" art. The large photographs in his office, Land said, were developed and framed for him after his comment to Ansel.

Ansel's work with Polaroid centered on the gray scale response of the film. Shades of gray could be adjusted to emphasize or minimize one or another feature of an image, and Ansel was expert in that ability. Many of his own spectacular photographs had been creatively modified in the darkroom, which was not an option with the Polaroid process, but he could comment on gray scale results in a Polaroid photo with authority.

Whether Land's comments about the importance of size were the first time Ansel heard them or not, he preferred a larger format for his work than the standard sizes for which Polaroid had sold millions of cameras. He encouraged Land to work with larger format, perhaps 5" x 9" film packages. He also taught a class or two in photography while he was in Cambridge. Hopeful students lined up in droves to take his course.

Ansel demonstrated in these brief visits his own forceful and unforgiving craftsmanship. On the one hand he was an approachable and pleasant grand-fatherly man, on the other an exacting technician.

Once we showed him the work of a photographer who was looking for a job, to ask him to criticize the work. Ansel focused on the way the work was presented: it was carelessly mounted on card stock. Ansel rejected the work and by inference the photographer himself, even before he got into more artistic issues.

I took his photography course and learned more about his values from that experience and from talking with his assistant. His images were usually quite realistic and carefully balanced: If a picket fence stood in front of a church building, he saw to it that the pickets lined up with the vertical lines of the church. A tree, if it was the subject, was complete to its topmost branches.

Images were also chosen for dramatic effect. Often his favorites showed its major subject in a rich gray. His assistant told me that one dramatic photograph, of a horse grazing in a field and illuminated by a strong ray of sunlight through a cloudy sky, required that his wife chase the horse about until it was lit correctly and then hide so that she wouldn't be photographed.

Ansel Adams in an Osborne Street doorway after lunch. He seemed to prefer eating with these folk rather than with lab personnel.

I photographed this wall of a seldom used room in a National Guard armory near MIT as a homework assignment in Ansel's class.

Of photos he requested as our class homework, he rejected one of mine that was arranged by hand as artificial and unreal (which it was), and liked one, unarranged, that showed a poster peeling off a plain gray wall.

He commented in his course on the tendency of viewers of photography to say something like "Do you see that face there? See? There are the eyes, the nose and, there, the mouth?" Ansel said more than one of his careful works had been ruined by such comments.

My responsibility was to manage his contract with Polaroid, hardly an onerous job. (He was paid $12,000 for his two weeks.) I saw to it that he got paid, arranged to pay a consulting fee for his assistant, acted as "registrar" for his course, and answered some of his infrequent questions.

I had by this time moved into one of the small offices in Land's anteroom which held a wonderful 30"x40'" Adams print. In response to my question, Ansel told me it would cost $400, too much for me.

As one Christmas approached, however, a loosely bound portfolio of Ansel's smaller photos sold at $75 for fifteen images. I found enough people who wanted these photos for $5 each as gifts to justify purchase and resale of two portfolios, and bought several photographs for myself. I asked Ansel about it after I had arranged the sale. He wasn't pleased. He said in his gentlemanly, modest manner that the 15 images in each portfolio were intended to be a coherent whole and not to be separated.

Later, in response to my written question, Sarah Adams, Ansel's granddaughter and in 1995 the Director of Fine Photography at the Ansel Adams Gallery in Pebble Beach, California, wrote me that if they were in good condition she could in her gallery ask about $4,000 for each. I had bought each for $5.

Other photographers showed up periodically. Paul Caponigro, now identified by Google as "one of America's most significant master photographers," did some contract work for Meroe. Nicholas Dean was a local professional who occasionally brought in wonderful photos.

One attractive young woman was employed almost full time as a photographer. We painted a wall on the roof of the building with lots of little segments in different colors, so she and others could demonstrate the accuracy of an experimental color film by comparing a photo of the wall with the original. She was also given assignments to test new black and white film types or speeds.

The Research

When a Polaroid camera took a picture, the image was first exposed to a silver emulsion-coated negative paper sheet. It and a sheet of positive paper with several layers of chemicals spread on it were then lined up together inside the camera. A small pod, held between the two sheets of paper, contained the carefully chosen chemicals that would activate the development of the image.

When the photographer first pulled the little sandwich out of the camera, it would be pulled between two steel rollers. The pod would burst and its viscous chemicals would spread evenly between the two sheets of paper. Transfer of the image from the negative paper to the positive began immediately and be completed in seconds.

Research in the process centered on the layers previously dried on the positive sheet and on the content of the little pod of chemicals. Eastman Kodak sold the negative sheet to Polaroid and so varying the negative material required contact with Kodak and was a ponderous act.

The laboratories developed a clever research device that allowed a small batch of chemicals to be mixed and inserted into an empty pod. Two syringes, similar to those used in medicine but lacking needles, were connected to each other by a small stainless steel nozzle. The chemicals were put in one of the syringes which then was connected to the other through the nozzle. The chemicals would be swished back and forth between the two syringes until they were well mixed. The mixture would be inserted into an empty pod and the three components (negative, positive and pod) put in a production camera and a picture taken for evaluation of that specific mixture.

Land insisted on the use of regular production cameras for the research, so that no variations in camera characteristics would enter into the research. The whole development process could thus be scaled up to the production level without undue complication.

A Polaroid camera as depicted in 1957.

When Polaroid introduced instant photography in 1947, the images were in sepia, not black and white. An important early research goal was to produce black and white images. In the search for the change, layers printed on the positive sheet and the chemicals in the pod could be varied and varied again. It was not so easy to change the composition of the negative sheet because Polaroid bought that material from Eastman Kodak. Changes in the negative material required contact with that firm.

A complete test in the laboratory thus went from the layers of chemicals on the positive sheet to the mixture of chemicals in the pod, to the resulting photograph and its analysis. Thus a complete test was a significant effort. Meroe met frequently with Land as they directed the work while technicians carried out the experiments and supervisors organized their work.

Meroe explained that she and Land approached the change from sepia to black and from different directions. She and a team of technicians started with the composition of the first of the layers spread on the photographic sheet; Land and another team started from the last; and each adjusted chemicals in the pod as they explored each change in the coatings. Technicians would prepare mixtures, assemble the little sandwiches, and take and evaluate one photo after another. They did this day after day, week after week, until finally they worked their way to the black and white image they sought. Polaroid's film was first described as "black and white" in the Company's 1950 annual report.

Meroe told me that the effort took 132,000 separate experiments. Thomas Edison is quoted as saying, "Success is 1 percent inspiration and 99 percent perspiration." That ninety-nine to one ratio was at least that high at Polaroid. The successful and complete Polaroid product certainly did not spring full-blown from anyone's mind.

Meroe seemed to me to be a touch embarrassed as she explained this remarkable effort. She believed — all of us believed — that Land was a genius. Yet, Land in his speech to MIT students years before had said, "He (a merely great man) will not suddenly say that mass is energy, that is genius." A popular impression of Land was that he perceived how to produce an instant image and "voila," it was done. I suspect Meroe, and perhaps Land himself, was chagrinned that it took so much empirical research over so much time to produce a finished and successful product.

In his efforts to keep researchers focused on such tedious work, Land frequently said that "here we are entitled to arrange events to our liking. Nature doesn't care how it comes out." Some independent researchers were free to make changes they felt were warranted so long as they also conformed to the specific tasks they were given. He used another comment, one of my favorites, to encourage a researcher downhearted at tedious failure after failure. "Success," he said, "is the end result of a series of failures."

Land explored his own interest in color through research conducted principally by Nigel Daw, a young Brit who had his own laboratory. The project dealt with making a color image through the interaction of two colors, not three, as in an ordinary color image.

An article in the website "eHow" by John Mack Freeman, contributor, describes the work and how Land came to it some years before:

"Land was attempting to create instant color photography by experimenting with three color projectors. After shutting off the green projector and removing the color from the projector, Land and his assistant noticed that, although only red and white light was being shown on the screen, they could see the whole range of colors where each would have appeared in the photograph being projected.

"Land tried a variety of experiments, usually using the colors of white and red to demonstrate that the full roster of hues in the spectrum can be seen using just these two color filters. Eventually he was able to show the full spectrum of color using two shades of yellow that were only 20 nanometers apart on the visible spectrum, and thus indistinguishable from one another to the naked eye. Although such images didn't have the value and boldness of printed images, the full range of colors was completely and obviously visible."

Thus, in other words, an image would be projected in slightly different shades of yellow onto a screen from two different projectors and the two images precisely aligned. Other colors - blues, reds, etc., - would be clearly visible, if somewhat faint. If one image was projected in red and the other in white and the images aligned precisely, all other colors would appear strongly. No wonder the experiment was an enthralling, even mystifying, one to see.

A common misconception was that this work and Howie Rogers' work on instant color film were the same. They were two separate projects and used different assumptions about color.

Nigel Daw conducted most of this unusual exploratory work without assistance, and the work was reported in "Scientific American" for May 1959, under the title "Experiments in Color Vision."

These experiments in color vision illuminate some of the attraction in working with Land: his ability to convey excitement. The first sentence of one article hints at an electrifying insight he and his researchers believed they had reached: "We have come to the conclusion that the classical laws of color mixing conceal great basic laws of color vision." No modest claim, that.

Again, from the "Scientific American" article: "No student of color vision can fail to be awed by the sensitive discernment with which the eye responds to the variety of stimuli it receives. Recently my colleagues and I have learned that this mechanism is far more wonderful that had been thought. The eye makes distinctions of amazing subtlety. It does not need nearly so much information as actually flows to it from the everyday world. It can build colored worlds of its own out of information materials that have always been supposed to be drab and colorless."

These theories did not collect immediate support from other researchers in the field of color. The ideas were criticized as not new, that the man (not Land) who had first reported them was not recognized, that the work was greatly misrepresented in importance, and that it was reported in an improper way by showing up in "Scientific American" as it did.

Land was troubled by the criticism and preferred describing his work to people who were willing to believe the experiments they saw rather than the comments of professionals.

Once he commented that the proper way to announce a new discovery was to bury it in a musty scientific journal. That way researchers would find it themselves and embrace it, and he could avoid the jealousy and criticism that would accrue from writing a sensational "Scientific American" article. I was told that Land or perhaps Nigel Daw found the first description of his work with two-color projection in just such a journal.

For the nonbelievers he struggled to find a way to commercialize the work. During my time at Polaroid Land's researchers tried to reduce this work in color vision to a practical product. He said that making a successful product was very hard to do, that it demonstrated how lucky the color film pioneers at Eastman Kodak and elsewhere were to have picked their three color, rather than a two color, process.

He argued that if people paid good money for something like a two-color process they would believe in it. At least one young woman tried to concoct a film type that could commercialize the work. She was scoring many very fine lines on a sheet of negative paper and filling them alternatively with different colors of light-sensitive compound and using the sheet in the photograph. Land said he would prove his case if he could sell it. She did not succeed.

An inconspicuous announcement in a dusty journal didn't fit with Land's personality. The research was too spectacular for quiet, scholarly revelation. He used the research, among his colleagues anyway, as evidence of one of innumerable areas outside of the classical academic disciplines in which a young person could contribute. His argument was perceived as one more mark of his genius.

The Mood

Land never, so far as I knew, described a potential researcher's job in other than general terms. His inclination seemed to be to talk with a new or prospective employee in glowing terms about the Company and the work they were to do, and put them to work, often under Meroe's tutelage. All would then wait to see how the new person fit in and how their performance affected the work.

Among Land's many endearing traits, he was contemptuous of "bureaucracy," an attitude that attracted young people. He reveled in irreverence for many of the trappings of normal working life. He was democratic in his own mannerisms, evocative in his comments and sometimes romantic and mysterious. Many people admired, even adored him.

This was a heady experience for a group of bright and believing young people. They were told they were revolting against the whole adult world of stuffy, disciplined, lingo-ridden academic science. His was sensuous language, appealing to beauty, to the glory of the body and to the unrealized and untapped potential of his listeners. Land would tell them they were seeing beautiful things and running important experiments no one in history had ever seen before. They were being told all this quite personally by a "genius," a remarkably successful and important man.

PRIVACY AND SECRECY

Often these researchers, particularly the young women, were told not to tell anyone what secret project they were working on. Several had private, lockable darkrooms of their own. The secrecy was no doubt in part to guarantee that no competitor or critic would be aware of what was going on. It also allowed Land to assign the same project to two different researchers simultaneously, or to allow him to try again when a researcher failed. His freedom to do as he wished was ensured if what he was doing was secret. In only one or two cases did I know in some detail specifically what a person was working on since few of them would describe their work and it wasn't appropriate to ask.

Nigel Daw described his work freely in the "Scientific American" article. It was colorful and easily explained, and seemed to be important. Nigel and Land even showed it off to the visiting President of the Japanese firm SONY. Visitors were treated to a display and to Nigel's careful description. They went away impressed.

The researchers were continually reminded of the glamour of the work. Land repeated often that they were part of a "revolution in photography." The wealth of the Company, its spectacular performance on Wall Street and all of Land's successes lent credence to such a statement. They saw distinguished visitors and Company Vice-Presidents waiting patiently for audience with him while he listened or worked with researchers. He was genuinely interested in their work and in them. They and their work were chosen over others with more important roles.

His researchers shared his glory as well, for Land was irrefutably a democrat. He was unfailing in his determination to credit the right person for an idea or a comment, even correcting other speakers as to the exact source of a comment. He seemed to respect the comments or insights of every individual without regard for their role or stature. It was an exhilarating place to work.

Some of Land's happiest moments seemed to come when one or another of these young women would report to him, complaining that their projects just didn't work. They might say, "It's not natural," or some variant. Land would repeat, "Nature doesn't care!" or perhaps, "We fail, fail, fail —that's our whole credo."

Land also had comments about the academic world, about which I think he had mixed feelings. On the one hand, in talking with him I felt he was very respectful of the physics department at MIT, about which I knew a little. On the other hand he would say that a field in science, a discipline, is simply the study of the accidental arrangement of events. "No one is a scientist, except the memory one holds of her teachers who know a little more about one subject than anyone else." If a researcher complained to him that she had no one to talk to, he would say that what she really means was that she can't confide in her professor and trust him to show her the answer.

Problems arose occasionally, of course. I remember one that dealt with a researcher's messiness. Once, when he was trying to encourage her to clean up her workspace to make it look more presentable, he pointed out in his positive manner: "Just straighten the edges of your piles of paper. It looks neat if the edges are neat."

I think Meroe did the serious discipline if such was needed, particularly in terms of relationships with Land or others. Land avoided unpleasant occasions and seemed particularly intent on avoiding situations where he had to say "No."

Meroe would handle complaints such as, "no one pays attention to me," if Land himself wasn't personally involved. Only once can I remember firing an employee, a male technician Meroe asked me to fire. The Company's effective personnel department handled complaints and legal problems. I think the usual solution for an employee unhappy with the work was simply to leave.

LATE NIGHT CRAM SESSIONS

An important but unusual rearrangement of laboratory work occurred periodically. The researchers, particularly the young women, would speak of these times as among the great experiences of working with Land.

When an important product needed particular emphasis, because it was near commercial sale, working conditions changed dramatically. Changes in the development chemicals, from those that reduced 60-second development of the photo to 10 seconds, precipitated such time changes. Working hours for researchers close to Land would be peremptorily disrupted, with late nights followed by the usual morning starting hours. These long hours would go on for perhaps a week or two, until the product was completely ready for commercial introduction. I was not directly involved in these sessions.

Land, with Meroe and other women working with him, would lead the work through the evening hours, sometimes until the small hours of the morning. Land would show up in the laboratory later in the morning, explaining that he was detained by corporate responsibilities he couldn't ignore. Because his office doors were soundproofed it was unclear whether or not he was in his office doing corporate work or just late to work. A visitor wouldn't know and his secretary wasn't telling.

One such marathon session was devoted to the introduction of a new camera. Different researchers were involved in this project. Many components of the new camera had to be brought to completion at the same time. We constructed a temporary shell of a room made of pegboard in a large unused space on the second floor. Each different component would get a marker ribbon which stretched along a horizontal string of holes in the pegboard.

One young woman had the responsibility of maintaining the markers. She would lengthen each marker, or not, as the project proceeded. An observer could tell quickly which parts of the project were on schedule or were falling behind simply by looking at the length of each marker compared to others.

Again, only certain people were allowed into the room. The work was for the people involved. The room stayed up longer than most cram sessions lasted but, as always, privacy and discretion prevailed.

PATENTS

Polaroid developed its patent system aggressively and effectively. Land knew of and approved every patent application sent from the Company. A corporate vice-president, a patent lawyer, was an occasional visitor to the labs as were one or two subordinates on his able and respectful staff. Generally young and zealous, the lawyers understood that their progress in the Company depended on the number and quality of issued patents. They went about their work diligently.

Land was extremely careful, even in everyday conversation, to recognize the originator of a phrase or an opinion, and certainly of a patentable idea. Whenever a new patent was issued, he, the lawyer responsible for the application and the inventor would meet for a little ceremony in Land's office, where a dollar bill would be cut in half. Land would get one half and the inventor the other. (Land's name might or might not be on the patent as well, but the Company would own it.) Both the lawyer and the inventor would get recognition, plus the thrill of meeting personally with the Company's famous president among all the spectacular Ansel Adams photos. It would be a memorable moment.

Land's attitude toward losing the monopoly in instant photography that Polaroid enjoyed was characteristic of his bravado. "By the time someone else develops a competitive product," he said, "we'll be so far ahead that it won't matter." The Company's strong patent system, nonetheless, gave Polaroid very important protection against competition.

Only Thomas Alva Edison had received more patents than Land had at the time, and currently (2011) Land is still fifth in the line of "top 10" patent recipients. Polaroid won a $925 million settlement from Kodak for patent infringement when Kodak introduced a competing instant camera and film. At the time this was by far the largest patent infringement award. Polaroid's vigorous development and defense of its patent systems paid off big time.

OTHERS ARE UNWELCOME

Land grew impatient quickly when one or another employee put numbers to his dreams. Salesmen were not welcome in the laboratories because they might, in their enthusiasm, calculate the sales potential or lack thereof of a product under development. Land insisted that the commercialism of sales and salesmen be kept out of the laboratories. He wanted to describe the potential of a product to a researcher himself. Numbers were suspect unless they were his own numbers in keeping with the dreams. In this sense he seemed more a Director of Research than a Company President. He supported research and researchers far more enthusiastically than he did sales and marketing or their people.

The blue doors and the mysterious corridor, plus the ubiquitous penchant for secrecy, did the job. The "innovative laboratories" maintained their freedom to think and dream without others, like pesky salesmen, setting limits or estimating a product's potential.

Diversification as a Laboratory Project

L and and his Board of Directors wanted to diversify the Company's product lines. His approach toward diversification often seemed to be to hire a promising employee and see if he or she could develop a role in the Company that would lead to diversification.

I know of two men hired in pursuit of a greater emphasis on physics and technology. One was a young and brilliant physicist, said to have an IQ of 180, who never seemed able to find a place in the Company. The other was a Washington, D.C., recruit hired at close to a Vice President's salary, ostensibly to develop a new physics laboratory. He was an employee intended, I believe, to fit more into the overall Company structure than into the photographic laboratories. I suspect Land hired him and waited to see what came of his job. Could he fit in the Company effectively? I think hiring these two employees were attempts to develop a Company role in digital photography. Neither employee succeeded and both left the Company.

Though Meroe talked of document copy as a trivial offshoot of photography, with its limited rendition of a photographic image, she considered it a logical way to increase the Company's product lines. Land ignored the opportunity for years, possibly considering it a distraction to more important work in photography. He did establish a document copy research and development effort later when, ultimately, he assigned the effort to me.

Land occasionally commented that he would be glad to support an able employee who wanted to develop a new business. He talked of the desire to fill a human need and to develop a product to meet that need. He saw instant photography as a product that fulfilled a basic human need. Perhaps he considered polarizing filters used in sunglasses and elsewhere as other such products.

Once, as he ate a lunch brought in by his secretary, he told me that what the world needed was a fat and juicy hamburger rather than the skimpy ones that fast-food franchises were selling. He implied he'd like to help an employee develop such a business.

He never, to my knowledge, showed any interest in purchasing another company in order to diversify Polaroid. To do so would have been inconsistent with his attitude toward Polaroid and its work. Polaroid was his creation, his invention, and any new business had to come from internal sources.

As a result of these human instincts, Polaroid never successfully diversified its product lines beyond cameras, film and polarizing filters.

My Work

My first serious responsibility as lab administrator was to develop a budget for laboratory expenses. This was a chore Meroe detested and had done begrudgingly, or not at all, in recent years. Budgetary estimates were developed by the Treasurer of the Company based on the previous year's expenses, modified a bit by salary and other expected increases, plus any new efforts he might learn about by asking Meroe or listening to Land.

The first full year I estimated that innovative laboratory expenses would be $1,100,000. The estimate was correct to within $1000.

I remember being asked only two questions about expenses after that, other than the inevitable, sometimes tendentious salary discussions about how much to pay different people in different branches of the Company. (Usually we faired well in those arguments for the labs were treated well.) The first question dealt with an expensive Single Lens Reflex camera that Meroe said Land wanted so as to compare images. An accountant called me, unhappy about the purchase, worried that the IRS might see that as a fringe benefit or perhaps as a gift for some employee. He might have been right; I never saw the camera.

The other question arose after I arranged to install the secure secret telephone to Washington in the basement under Land's office with its handset on his desk. The principal Corporate Operating Officer called to complain about the cost. The government should pay for that, he argued. I didn't have any idea how that could be done and neither he nor I wanted to ask Land. Ultimately we just added the cost to laboratory expenses.

"Fortune" magazine quoted Land as saying, "He wants Polaroid to be known as the first manufacturer in the world that recognized the human dignity of every employee all day long." He said he wanted employees to alternate periods of routine work with periods in a creative research environment. He wanted every employee to spend an hour a day in class or in learning opportunities the Company made available. He talked of these efforts as a crusade against all the insensitive bureaucratic characteristics of other corporations.

This ambition of his wasn't as much in contrast with the characteristics of other companies as argued. Polaroid was hardly the first manufacturer to claim to recognize human dignity. I spent an hour a day, on average, in classroom work or in educational programs when later I worked for some years at the General Electric Company. This was much more time than I spent doing similar things at Polaroid.

Work in the innovative photographic laboratories, however, was one way Land felt human dignity could be expressed. On one occasion, additional lab technicians were needed. I spent a week interviewing 60 production workers seeking men and women I felt could fit into the lab environment.

Within a few weeks twelve of the 60 were transferred to the laboratories. There was no concern for the expense because the lab work was important. There was little concern about the jobs they left because they could be filled with new applicants. Morale of employees on the production line was reported to have soared. Land's promises about human dignity or at least a chance to work in the innovative laboratories seemed to have been fulfilled.

Questions of construction and space, another of my work responsibilities, came up when research demands increased. Land and Meroe decided on one occasion to enlarge her laboratory. I spent two weeks drawing up plans for a new second floor lab.

Had a digital camera taken this photo of me I could erase the cigarette. I had no such luck with a Polaroid photo. It wasn't nearly that easy to erase the habit!

Land heard my ideas, looked at my drawings, and then took charge, ignoring my plans completely. He said, in discussing another, much bigger and grander construction project that others were urging upon him, that "the monumental is enemy to the fundamental." He really liked the wooden floors and marginally decrepit conditions of his old furniture factory. Though I had respected those features in my plans for a new laboratory, he wanted it done differently.

For this new laboratory he brought Company construction engineers into the space, saying that "certain fundamental work had reached the stage where it needed more space quickly." He walked through the area with the engineers, pointing here and there. He wanted a sink here, a darkroom there. He asked them to mark these items on the bare wooden floors with chalk. They were told to estimate the cost and build the facilities simultaneously.

When the work was finished, two weeks later, it proved to be both economical and exciting for the engineers. They had just circumvented typical bureaucratic procedures. "Nothing like working with the big Boss," they reported. "He gets things done!" I also learned a lesson on how to get a project done at Polaroid: get Land personally involved.

I spent most of my working time as an administrator in an office I shoe horned into a widened corridor until I was assigned an office in Land's anteroom and, later, my own laboratory and machine shop. More about that later.

A Harem?

The presence of such a collection of attractive women, some of them young and unmarried, raised questions about their purpose in the laboratories. I was teased that I was maintaining a harem. The soundproofing doors and the locked darkrooms stimulated rumors: Why soundproof office doors? Had one of the women raised a ruckus over a relationship with Land? Why lock a darkroom? A visitor can knock before barging in or a light saying "IN USE" could discourage interruption and would be safer than a locked door in case of accident. I also heard the old joke, "Let's go in the darkroom and see what develops," many times. Other than the one anecdote I'll relate, however, I had no personal experience with the issue.

The rumors of a harem traveled well. I suspect the employees who had known Land for years thought the rumors were true. Dr. Killian, by then back at MIT, was on the Polaroid Board of Directors for a while. I occasionally called on him for a brief conversation. Once he asked if the rumors about Land's relationship with these women were true. I said I thought there was some truth to them but I was confident they'd be kept quiet. (I knew Meroe was very effective in maintaining discipline and discretion.) Dr. Killian wasn't happy with that answer but never asked me again.

I didn't know what went on during the marathon late-night cram sessions that preceded a new product introduction, except that they ended as quickly as they began, when the product was introduced.

My one direct experience came in a conversation with one of the young women, a good friend. We often talked frankly with one another; she described her work to me in detail. We were talking about the intense lab work in the current late night cram session, which had gone on for several days.

She told me that Land had shown up at her door about 9 pm the previous evening to say he loved her. I didn't ask what happened next. I guess I'll never know.

Conversations

I can remember a phrase or two that surprised me as Land talked. The comments would fall into my category of "grandstanding." I suspected their purpose might have been to impress and display to others his keen perceptive ability, but the differences he identified were so small his comments weren't credible. He pointed out distinctions that existed but that I felt were too small to be apparent.

Once Meroe, Land and I walked together into the Kresge auditorium at MIT where he was to give a speech. The composition floor of the entryway contained thousands of tiny crystalline flecks of mica imbedded in the flooring material. Their sparkle caught his eye. "They look different from one eye than from the other," he said. They had to; the tiny crystals reflected light slightly differently to one eye than to the other because each eye looked at them from a slightly different angle.

It may be that he meant just that, if you studied the sparkles intently with one eye and then the other (perhaps by photographing them first from the perspective of one eye and then from the other) one could find differences. It would be difficult, however, even working from photos taken at eye level a couple inches apart. As a quick observation I felt it was impossible.

At the time all I could manage was the response, "Good thing Galileo didn't have that problem."

As a defense to the legitimacy of the comment, however, Land won a Presidential Medal of Honor for his work in aerial reconnaissance. Looking down at sparkling bits of mica in a floor could be considered a trivial example of aerial reconnaissance. Perhaps it was just an example of the "inspiration" that Edison called "1 percent" of genius. Who am I to doubt him?

Another similar comment surprised me. He showed several of us a photograph taken by a unique camera. It had four lenses contained within the same aperture and took four different photos of a face with one exposure. Because of the geometry of the lens, each face had to be slightly different because each was taken at a very slightly different angle from the others.

Land said you could see the difference. They were different, of course, but it wouldn't be easy to distinguish differences in four images of the same face some distance away when the photos were taken simultaneously and only millimeters apart.

My sense, in both these examples and others, was that Land was making distinctions that had to exist but that weren't nearly as evident as he implied. The apparent ability to make such distinctions added to his reputation.

Throughout my tenure at Polaroid the introduction of instant color film was an eagerly awaited event, both within the Company and, we believed, throughout the photo-taking world. Another conversation stands out that dealt with that subject.

The anecdote demonstrates the popular anticipation for color film. Once when I was sitting in Land's anteroom he burst out of his office door laughing. He had just finished a conversation with a "Texan" who wanted to buy a roll or two of color film, for his daughter, as I recall. Land told him that the film had not been introduced but would be available shortly. They apparently argued a bit and the caller, frustrated, finally asked, "How much do you want for your itty-bitty company?" Land was delighted.

I occasionally spent an hour or so in Land's office talking with him about the Company and his philosophies. I was able to speak frankly, perhaps even encouraged to do so. Once I told Land I had heard that employee morale on the production lines was low. Polaroid wanted very much to avoid unionization of its work force so a comment on morale could be important. A week or so later he had production-line employees brought together on the factory floor and repeated for them the exciting things he believed about the

Company. Land repeated such meetings for different employee groups two or three times.

During another conversation, he surprised me with a comment I still can't understand. I must have expressed some criticism or other and, I suspect, hit a nerve. "Aren't you proud of me?" he asked. From a man old enough to be my father and the subject of both widespread and personal admiration, the question still rings in my head. "Aren't you proud of me?"

Power Struggle

In February, 1962, Land invited me to sit in on the weekly meetings of the Company's "Operating Policy Committee." The Committee was composed of the Vice-Presidents, the Treasurer, a Corporate Secretary, and Land. A contemporary of mine, an Assistant Secretary, took the minutes. I was there, apparently, just as an observer. This experience gave me far greater insight into what was really going on with color film.

The Committee's attention at the time was focused on a controversy between two Vice-Presidents about the introduction of the new instant color film. The controversy became a major power struggle ostensibly between Bob Casselman, Sales VP, and Stan Calderwood, Advertising VP.

Casselman was the senior VP of the two and had a long and successful connection with the Company. He seemed the very model of a corporate chieftain: self-confident, competitive, assertive and willing to challenge anyone's authority. Calderwood was the younger of the two and, to my mind, more accessible and imaginative. I believe the meetings of the Committee had begun some four months before I was invited to sit in, to air this controversy in front of all the Corporate officers.

Land let both men explain their positions at some length and the controversy went on for several meetings. Polaroid had to proceed one way or the other: Casselman's way or Calderwood's. The resolution of the struggle had a significant effect on the future of both men.

Calderwood, and Land himself, wanted color film to be introduced nation-wide with a promotion that would gather national attention and response. This was effectively the way a new film had been introduced when the Company improved developing time from sixty seconds to ten. While instant color film was a more important venture than that, Calderwood saw no drawbacks to repeating the plan except a possible, and understandable, delay as supplies became available everywhere.

Casselman, the Sales VP, suggested a different approach. He wanted color film introduced region by region, starting in Florida and distributing product to camera owners by mail from Cambridge. Polaroid had sold about 4 million cameras, but many were seldom used after the owners' initial excitement. Casselman wanted to contact each owner directly, to sell them their first roll by mail along with detailed instructions on its use and inviting them to send their cameras back to be renovated. Distribution would continue that way, region by region, until the film was available everywhere.

Casselman argued that there were advantages to his plan. Contacting all owners would emphasize dramatically how much Polaroid cared about its owners and would as well get many cameras off closet shelves and back into use. Owners would get clear instruction on the use of the film. The plan could be started and stopped quickly, if problems arose. It would also, not incidentally, produce a good new mailing list for sales use.

As others pointed out, it could also give Casselman almost complete control of the channels of product distribution. Polaroid by this time had about 14,000 distributors, some of whom had been troublemakers for the sales department. Polaroid products were a source of a significant share of their sales. They looked forward to instant color film as a new and profitable source of income. If Casselman chose, should the Company follow his regional plan, he could continue to sell color film directly from Cambridge and possibly cut distributors, and their profits, out of color film entirely. Such a plan would be a major change in the Company's approach to sales.

The differing attitudes of the two men seem easy to understand. Calderwood, as Advertising VP, wanted to gain as much publicity out of this major product introduction as possible. Color Polaroid film was already anticipated widely and its actual availability was a nationally important event.

I believe Casselman had different motives. He was quoted once as arguing that the magic that made Polaroid was not so much the instant development of a finished photo as that the product's availability coincided with the dramatic growth in popularity and acceptance of television. The Company's success was not so much due to an innovative product as to the effective way it was marketed.

A Polaroid commercial in the late 40s was certainly a noteworthy event. Watching an instant photograph taken and developed on television commanded attention. "Will it really work?" When it did, viewers could believe the product was real and reliable. Sales boomed.

Casselman, I was told, felt that those commercials and their excitement sold the camera; that the Company was essentially driven by sales and not by clever products. He was confident and competitive enough to argue that sales, not innovation, accounted for the success of the Company.

I also felt that he didn't completely trust the new product and had as well seen the successful use of regional introductions as the Company went national with its first camera. When it was first introduced in Boston, in 1947, the Company had only 4 or 5 dozen cameras available, calculating they would have time to replace the stock as those sold. They had to mount a major manufacturing effort and quickly establish many dealerships, but they also had time to modify the product as they went along.

By now they had 4 or 5 million cameras out. Regional, slower introduction would give the Company time to adjust and to correct any problems with the product and, perhaps, to test various sales techniques.

Land asked about the logistics of sending out four or five million letters, responding to them and then responding to the responses. Casselman would say "We can do that. It's not a problem." He wouldn't back down.

I feel in many ways the real power struggle was between Casselman and Land himself, not between the two Vice-Presidents. Casselman credited salesmanship with the products' great success and felt that Polaroid was, and should be. a sales dominated Company. Land and Calderwood credited the products.

The argument went on for some time. The Operating Policy Committee met weekly but, in the meantime, the production of the film, its availability, and its introduction to the public came closer and closer.

After several meetings Land told me by telephone I wasn't to attend any longer. I may have been invited to the meetings, by him, to learn my reaction to the controversy and so as we talked I told him I thought that Calderwood's plan was much more sensible. The struggle, I argued, merited a realignment of the authority of the two VPs so that it could be implemented. I didn't realize that the showdown was to come at the meeting I was told not to attend.

Right after the meeting Calderwood was promoted to Sales VP. Casselman was reassigned to directing a laboratory concerned with the promotion of medical X-ray photography, another potential way to diversify the Company. The Company introduced color film nationally as Calderwood proposed.

The solution was presented as an opportunity for each, but it was clearly a promotion for Calderwood and a demotion for Casselman. Land resolved the controversy without saying "no" to either man. Both were given new jobs.

Land had no doubt talked it all out at length with Meroe, Howie Rogers, and his Board, and perhaps privately with one or two of the other Vice-Presidents. Resolution of the argument resolved the power struggle and, at the same time, confirmed Land's domination of the Company as a product-driven, not sales-driven, Company.

Stockholders See the Film

Public introduction of the film was scheduled to occur at the 1963 annual meeting of stockholders. The event had to be done right. Land and Howie Rogers and others had worked for years to see this moment. Production facilities were in place and public anticipation was high. We spent some time talking about how to display the product successfully at the meeting. How should we introduce it?

One idea we considered was to create a number of colorful domestic scenes to be photographed. Stockholders could be lent cameras and encouraged to take their own photos, of a family gathered around a dinner table as the Thanksgiving turkey is brought in, for example, or perhaps children playing on a colorful swing set. That idea was dropped, however, and a different one chosen.

The chosen presentation required the work of laboratory people. Land asked me to work it out, and Meroe, Inge Reithof, and others took important roles. We were to collect or take ourselves a great many attractive color photos using ordinary cameras and the film we were about to sell. All of us were to use production film and production cameras, so the photographs would be just like camera owners would take themselves.

I was about to take a vacation in Colorado with my family when the project came up, so I took my camera and took photos, some above timberline. A colorful photo taken at that altitude demonstrated film versatility, which was a goal in collecting photos of different subjects and scenes and in varying conditions.

One spacious room in the production factory had yet to be outfitted with production machinery. Crews set up a podium and loudspeaker system and a number of folding chairs. Crews hung gray floor-to-ceiling drapes near the walls all around the large room. Hundreds of visitors were expected.

Inconspicuous wires and hooks were hung in front of the gray drapes. We carefully mounted eight of our photos on many 2x8 foot gray panels and hid the panels and their photographs on the floor behind the drapes. Spotlights were affixed to the ceiling. (Land had them moved back and forth until he was satisfied that the pictures were at eye level and properly illuminated when hanging in front of the drapes. It was reminiscent of the photos hung in the dark corridor near his office.) Before the meeting a sizeable crew of production workers hid behind the curtains next to the gray panels.

The audience was admitted to huge room and, after the usual milling around, took their seats. Land opened the meeting with a report on the status of the Company, gave other reports, and then reminisced at some length about the development of instant color film. He identified and credited Howie Rogers and others involved with the development of the film. Then he said, as I recall, "I guess it's time."

The lights went out, the room went black instantly, and the corps of workers picked up and hung the panels in front of the gray drapes. Spotlights went on a moment later to illuminate hundreds of beautiful color photos hanging on panels all around the room. Land invited the audience to examine the photos. They did so, excitedly and with much chatter.

Thus did Land and Polaroid introduce color film.

Document Copy

My life at Polaroid took a dramatic turn after the color film introduction. I was assigned a new office, oversight of a machine shop and a film laboratory, each with its own manager, and a totally new role. I was to get Polaroid into the document copy business.

I knew that Land had tried to diversify the product line of the Company several times. Cameras and film were the overwhelming money-makers, with polarizing filters and sunglasses a distant second. The Company needed to diversify its product line and add another important product. It needed a new business. Document copy seemed to offer just such an opportunity.

Land and Meroe believed that making a copy of a document was easy, almost a no-brainer when compared with the demands of a photograph. Film technology could lend itself to document copy without much effort. After all, a copy of a business letter need only be black and white; there was little need to worry about shades of gray. Just take a picture of a sheet of paper, develop the image and spew out a finished product.

Land was the innovator at Polaroid, not his Vice-Presidents. I don't believe he trusted, or for that matter wanted, any of them to develop a new product. In one of our conversations he called the Vice-Presidents "a rum bunch." He had seen and dealt with controversies among them and I believe disliked the arguments. His Vice-Presidents each had his own role. Introduction of a new product was not one of them.

Land didn't need his Vice-President's approval for a new course of action, for he owned 20% of the Company's stock and had final say on almost everything. However, he wanted their support for a new product, regardless of their role in developing it. I was accepted well enough by now that a new document copy business could be understood as coming out of his laboratories, and not from some VP's area. They would give it their supporting effort.

I was outfitted for this project with a laboratory with tables, a darkroom, running water and working space. A properly equipped machine shop with its manager was next door. I bought an easy chair similar to those I know Land liked for his use to put in my office. I expected occasional conversations with him about the project.

Thus prepared we embarked. The goal was to develop a photocopy machine that would be a comfortable addition to anyone's desk, perhaps on top of it like a typewriter or standing next to it like a two drawer file cabinet. The machine would copy an 8 1/2 x 11 inch sheet of paper cleanly, with as little effort as possible for the user. The copy should be cheap, stable, dry quickly and, of course, be a completely accurate black and white rendition of the original. Considering all the constraints of photographing, developing and producing a copy of the original and disposing of the waste, the design became complex.

There were important complications. We were seriously late and had to catch up. Xerox had already introduced a product that made satisfactory copies quickly with little or no pretreatment of the copy paper.

The need to catch up with Xerox was to me the major issue. Xerox had introduced its "914" copy machine and was pioneering the document copy business. Polaroid installed one of the Xerox machines in its offices across Osborne Street, and the machine's usefulness grew daily. Put an original on a glass plate, push a button and a sharp black and white copy emerged quickly. Xerox used no silver, just a black "toner" that would fuse quickly with heat onto a sheet of ordinary paper. They claimed a good copy could be made even on a Kraft paper bag. The gray ranges of a photograph didn't reproduce very satisfactorily, but ordinary business correspondence didn't need a sophisticated range of grays. Already a river of paper was flowing through Xerox machines.

Eastman Kodak had already introduced a silver-based product using their trademark, "Verifax," that would copy documents satisfactorily. It required the user first to expose the original, separate two moistened sheets of paper by hand, and finally to dispose of the waste. The product wasn't doing very well.

Ours, using a silver coated negative, would also require developing liquid to be spread between two sheets of paper which, after development, would be separated in the machine. The used negative sheet had to be disposed of carefully. Reports of used negatives from camera film littering scenic areas embarrassed Land. Document copy would use much larger sheets of negative than cameras and so had to be disposed of carefully.

The use of a silver emulsion was an important issue. Silver was an expensive precious metal. Every bit of silver would add to the cost of the product, which had to be as inexpensive as possible.

Producing our own paper negative would allow Land to realize a dream, to manufacture our own emulsion coated paper. If Polaroid made its own they would no longer be dependent on Eastman Kodak. A successful document copy business would use great quantities of such paper and would propel the Company into the manufacture of its own negative materials.

I wrote an extensive report on the characteristics we needed for our machine and on the vigorously expanding and competitive document copy business. Xerox dominated the market and other firms offered other technologies. I believed our product needed to be introduced quickly if it had any chance to succeed. We were trying to introduce a new horse drawn buggy after automobiles had replaced them.

I asked Land to work on document copy vigorously and personally. Our effort needed a technological breakthrough and I believed that Land could provide it if he focused directly on the problem. However, the only technical suggestion I remember his making was one I had heard in other contexts. For a problem separating individual sheets of paper, which was then still a possibility for our machine, we should make an octopus-like device with arms and suction cups to lift one sheet from the one below it.

I never got a direct answer to my request for greater involvement. I think he expected me to develop the product with the help I had, turning to him for advice now and then. After all, Howie Rogers had done that in color film. He had proceeded slowly and deliberately, and had succeeded. I should do the same. Land was willing to wait.

Instead of saying "No" he and Meroe held an unusual meeting in the Company library where he told the assembled engineers and scientists that color film needed maximum effort from all concerned to be certain the product introduction continued satisfactorily.

I believed that meeting was held for my benefit, that the chosen audience of researchers and engineers was not the right one for such a message. Color film was by now in the hands of manufacturing and marketing groups. If total effort was to be devoted to color film, he implied that other research, on document copy or whatever, had to be a distant second.

The trouble was, document copy and I couldn't wait. Land didn't want to tell me that he wasn't going to focus on document copy. I believe he felt that he had already established focus enough. Just tell everyone, me included, that something else is more important and he wouldn't have to say "No" to me. I'd get the point.

I Quit

I told Land a day or two later that I could not do the job in document copy and that I was leaving the Company. I didn't explain my reasons beyond that nor was I asked about them. I was in no mood to hear his idealistic pep talk about the difficulty of our work, or whatever, so I simply quit.

"It's well known that I'm difficult to work for," he said. "All right." That was that.

I moved out of my office, took a desk in another building and spent several weeks of part-time secretarial work searching for a job elsewhere. I never went behind the blue doors again, to my friends and working home of more than four years. I wasn't welcome.

I'm sure that Meroe was upset at my leaving. She had been my champion. I made an attempt to see her some time after I left the Company, but a satisfactory meeting time could never be arranged. She never said "No," just that she couldn't make any of the times I suggested.

Polaroid never introduced a product in document copy. Looking over two patents related to document copy that were issued in my name after I left, the patent drawings make the machine look like an elaborate "Rube Goldberg" device, full of wheels and other devices. Short of some totally different concept than we had to work with, however, such design was unavoidable.

A friend at Harvard Business School told me some years later that Polaroid spent about $225,000,000 on its aborted effort to get into document copy. My friend consulted with Polaroid and should know, but I find that amount surprising. I spent only a tiny fraction of that, about $15,000 a month, on the dozen or so people who worked for me on the original design. Completing the design and then scaling a product up to a production level would probably cost millions, but not such a surprising sum.

The Company spent an enormous amount, if my friend's figure is correct, on developing the desired emulsion-making competence. I can think of no other way the Company could have spent such a large sum on document copy. It was an expensive decision.

From a Distance

After all that intense involvement with an "authentic genius," I have reflected many times on the man and his work. I recall my feelings when I left Polaroid and while in many respects they haven't changed, they have been modified and enriched by my life since then.

Polaroid grew and changed a lot after I left. Many things happened in which I had no involvement whatsoever. They include the substantial patent infringement award won by Polaroid from Eastman Kodak, the continued sales growth, Land's removal as President and, of course, the Company's ultimate bankruptcy.

Film photography has been replaced by digital photography. The photography business has become primarily an electronics business. Many people are saddened by the demise of an effective, almost romantic form of image creation, just as some were saddened by the change from horse-drawn buggies to automobiles.

Fuji in Japan bought Polaroid's instant photography business. Niche markets for instant film photography still exist, in driver's licenses and passport photos, for example, because they cannot be as easily modified as can digital images. Film photography, however, is about as obsolete as horse-drawn buggies. Such a development colors any assessment of Polaroid's "authentic genius."

Thomas Edison was instrumental in founding General Electric, now one of the largest companies in the world. Edison's broad legacy extends beyond General Electric and includes far more than a handful of product lines. Alexander Graham Bell's invention of the telephone far outlasted the man himself, and it too spawned a whole bevy of big companies.

Land's major contribution, important as it was, succumbed about the time as did the man himself. His film technology, the change in a silver salt when it was exposed to light, was just not broad enough. It has not carried much beyond his original application, unlike the offspring of the Edison or Bell technologies.

If Land's response to his daughter's question, "why do we have to wait so long" qualifies as "inspiration," Land clearly added "perspiration" and worked vigorously and at great lengths to realize the dream of a quickly produced photograph. If Edison's definition of genius is correct, 1 percent inspiration and 99 percent perspiration, Land qualifies as a genius.

A common criticism of Land says that he never diversified the Company. That was not for lack of trying. Rather, he was out of contact with the larger world of image creation and didn't associate with sales people or others who could have kept him informed. He lived in and was limited by his own research success.

A well-known example of his attempt to diversify was a product introduced in 1977 named "Polavision." The very expensive system, film, camera and projector, made a short motion picture film that could be displayed quickly but was introduced about the same time as were electronic home-movie making systems with their VHS and Betamax alternatives. Polavision failed quickly and expensively. The event reportedly led to Land's removal as President.

That failure preceded the Company's failure with document copy, which is not so well known publicly. The earlier failure must have been a source of embarrassment for the Company, if not for Land himself. I doubt, though, that the failure of Polavision by itself led to his dismissal, though it must have made his judgment questionable.

I have often wondered if other authorities at Polaroid (such as the Board or the VP of Engineering) didn't stop the commercial introduction of document copy because it would simply repeat that earlier failure. Document copy had already cost nearly a quarter of a billion dollars. The product as presented, I believe, was an awkward and expensive alternative to the elegant Xerox product, and the commercial introduction of such a product was probably condemned to failure.

The money spent on document copy might also have perfected Polaroid's own emulsion, a matter of pride and loyalty to Land and his employees, but that would not be true diversification. It would simply broaden the Company's commitment to instant photography. A second expensive failure to diversify, another flop like Polavision, would be a serious mistake.

Land's ultimate failure lay in trying to diversify simply by replicating his own success in photography without directing serious effort to the more broadly changing world of image formation. It may not have been possible to make a truly broad change in the Company. No other redirection of its efforts succeeded, however.

Land described Polaroid in glowing terms, as the very essence of a desirable employer, one where every individual was helped to develop to his or her full potential, where each employee spent at least an hour a day in class or in learning new things. It was a Company engaged in work at the evocative "interface of science and art." Perhaps Land hoped that by describing an ideal company his associates and employees — me included — he could make the grand ideas come true. Work in the "innovative labs" had some of these characteristics, but I think the Company as a whole was quite ordinary in its management practices.

I feel that his genius lay principally in his ability to enthuse and involve others. The bright and attractive people around him — Meroe Morse was a characteristic example — were completely and totally involved in the research he asked them to do. The results were exciting products and accomplishments that energized them and provided good jobs, made money for him and the Company, and added luster to his reputation. These people added far more "perspiration" to the definition of genius than one man could provide alone.

I list the Company's failure with document copy along with other failures, including that of the young woman who worked to develop a two-color film and the introduction of Polavision. Failures, large and small, were not uncommon at Polaroid. I suspect they might have been less overwhelming, maybe even avoided, had Land been more receptive to the ideas and insights of others, particularly sales people.

The Company introduced the first feature length, full-color, three-dimensional film "Bwana Devil" in 1952, viewed through alternatively polarized, inexpensive plastic 3-D glasses. Polaroid's efforts failed because of the difficulties in getting two slightly different images, projected by two different projectors, to coincide precisely on every theater screen. Watching these early 3-D films was uncomfortable and led many to headaches.

Polaroid also tried for years to get the auto industry to accept polarizing filters for use on automobiles. They would have the same glare-reducing properties as polarizing sunglasses. Nighttime or rainstorm driving would be better illuminated and its glare reduced, if all cars had polarized windows. Detroit never accepted the product. Gradually the Company dropped its efforts to commercialize such a product.

The demise of film photography and the Company's bankruptcy freeze Land's major contributions at his work with instant photography, cameras, polarizing filters and military photography. No one else commercialized his most successful innovation, instant photography, to the extent Polaroid did. No one else profited so substantially from it as did Polaroid. No one else built upon silver technology as they did on electricity or telephones.

Land's inspiring words enthused researchers and painted a glowing picture of an ideal corporation, one where we'd all like to work. Land was marvelous as a "Director of Research," his preferred title among the three he held: President, Chairman of the Board and Director of Research. Within the boundaries he established, it was also the one job he did well.

"Success is the end result of a series of failures," he would say. Land's story is far more about his successes and his methods than about his failures; even more about his words and dreams than about film photography. Working for him was a grand adventure. He was an enthralling and extraordinary man.

Epilogue

2013

This Life Goes On

After the Polaroid experience I spent two years in the General Electric Company as Manager of Paint Product Development at an anachronistic paint business in Chelsea, Mass. GE has since sold the business but, at the time, it broadened GE's offerings as another way to apply electric insulation. My predecessor in the job had been fired and left a lot of commonplace but uncompleted tasks to be done by his replacement.

During my two years the business grew 44 percent in sales to 9 percent in profitability, both unusually good statistics for an established commodity business like paint. I wrote an article about the use of computers in product design that won a paint industry award. I was promoted to a higher level job in Schenectady and was ultimately offered a job with the Chairman of the GE Board, as a way, I believe, of being introduced to GE's various divisions and businesses. I didn't want to work for yet another famous man and, besides, I saw an opportunity to get back into the academic world.

John F. Kennedy, in his Presidential inaugural address, said, "There is nothing we cannot do in a host of new cooperative ventures." JFK's "we" was the US and the Soviet Union, but many college people took it as good advice, and I profited. The President of Union College, the supervisor of a friend of mine, was charged with finding a director to establish a cooperative organization of private colleges of the NY Capital District. I contacted him.

In 1966 and 1967 I interviewed 9 local Capital District private college presidents. After making the rounds twice, they hired me to establish an organization that would promote cooperation among them. Named "Hudson-Mohawk Association of Colleges and Universities," ultimately the region's two public community colleges, its public university and another private college, Maria College, joined the group.

Over the years we established cooperative purchasing agreements which saved millions of dollars and built upon the well-known benefits of scale. RPI bought thousands of gallons of fuel oil annually, for example, and the business manager told me initially that they had negotiated the best price possible. We found, to his surprise, that RPI was paying more than was Union College, a smaller consumer. Joined together with others in a single purchase contract, however, both benefitted.

We established other important cooperative programs. We published a newsprint periodical listing all local college continuing education courses every term. We surveyed students twice and found many who first learned of a continuing education opportunity from our publication. We arranged for students from one member college to take a course or two at another college, without extra cost, if the chosen course was not available at their home campus. We developed programs in admissions and in the arts. We set up a study-abroad program in Seville. Only one or two of these efforts to draw similar administrators together failed. Development officers, concerned with their own campus data and resources, weren't interested in sharing. Athletic coaches had their own systems for contact with others.

I did this for seventeen years and grew to believe that most people in the business of college cooperation pursued approaches that were counterproductive. One such approach was to seek outside grant money. Providers of such money usually want financial commitment from the cooperating colleges. That willingness to provide that money can differ widely among colleges. A financial requirement sometimes lead to estranged member colleges that didn't want to be committed to support a cooperative project in which they weren't interested.

I found that I could work out cooperation among a few colleges at a time and that getting all to cooperate on anything was unusual. (Our annual "College Fair," which invited colleges all over the country to Albany for a day and arranged for great numbers of local high school seniors to meet them, was of no interest at all to Albany Law School or other graduate institutions. On the other hand, the Law School was very interested in cooperative purchasing.) My challenge was to involve each college in projects enough to justify their membership in our cooperative organization.

I dealt with the college presidents carefully and involved them only peripherally. I worked under 35 different college presidents during my seventeen years at the job. I met with the presidents, of course, and called on each of them at least once a year, but except for a ritualistic annual dinner I was never keen on getting them together. They could manage their own colleges successfully. I was afraid of what they might mandate if they decided to manage my organization.

The principal method of operating I chose was to gather administrators with similar jobs together in my office, to get them away from their offices for a lunch I provided. The Admissions Officers, Registrars, Purchasing Agents and other groups thus met others doing their job on another campus. These men and women usually had cooperative ideas they could agree upon. I usually would take away some task or other from the meeting, and they could talk freely with others about their jobs, their bosses and other features of their job. Then in my formal meetings with the Presidents I would detail agreements and accomplishments, and point to specific examples of cooperation.

One of the cooperating colleges, the Albany Medical College, asked me to join various medical advisory groups. The request led me to an entirely new line of work. Part-time for 30 years, both while at the Association and after my retirement in 1986, they arranged for me to be a governor-appointed, non-physician member of the "NY State Board for Professional Medical Conduct." Five or six of us worked on details of its formation in the mid-seventies, including the State Health Commissioner, several MDs and Health Department staff plus, at arm's length, the NY State Legislature and the State's Medical Society.

I chaired the Board for two years in the 1980's and over the years took part in disciplining many hundreds of physicians, including many whose licenses were revoked.

Medical "misconduct" is not medical "malpractice," though the two categories often overlap. Charges of misconduct are prosecuted by the State through our Board, while malpractice is usually brought by an individual and is prosecuted in the courts. The former might be suspected insurance fraud or a charge of selling drug prescriptions, while the latter is often a perceived medical error.

A common misconduct scenario could involve an immigrant MD with a new NY medical license who got caught up in a Medicaid mill. As a licensed MD he might have signed many insurance claims his employer put before him, for patients the MD never saw. The employer would then submit the claims for reimbursement. Our job was to judge the extent of the dishonesty, from unknowing naiveté to glaring complicity, and decide on an appropriate discipline.

We also judged occasional sex abuse cases. An interesting example demonstrates two feature of abuse: a somewhat limited young woman called a popular talk show host to ask if it was sex abuse when a doctor she named had her, in her initial exam, crawl naked around the room on hands and knees. Did the talk show host think this was abuse? Several other women heard the broadcast and independently brought their own charges of sex abuse against the MD. Because they came forward and spoke in support of the original victim, the case changed abruptly from a "he said, she said" controversy into one of serial abuse.

In his defense the MD called a beautifully dressed and confident woman in her 40s who, after throwing her fur coat casually on a chair, testified that the MD was marvelous, that he couldn't possibly abuse a woman. The case dramatized for me that an abusing MD would often focus on vulnerable women. The woman who testified on his behalf was hardly a vulnerable woman; the women who testified against him, including the first, were troubled in one way or other.

Sex abuse against a man was rare, though not missing entirely. One man and his wife, suspicious of his MDs behavior, claimed that when the man was under sedation the doctor performed a sex act on him. The wife, hiding in a closet, burst out when she perceived the doctor starting a sex act on her husband and beat on him with a broom. They then reported the case to our Board.

I was President of the volunteer Albany League of Arts and, finally and sadly, the President of a newly merged Albany and Schenectady arts groups. I chaired the first organization twice, helped it and the Schenectady group merge. A lesson: If two organizations are each having trouble, joining them together may just make the trouble bigger. Both of these organizations had serious money shortfalls. Merging them didn't help much. Nor did I, in months of trying.

We then saw NY State Attorney General Eliot Spitzer pick the merged organization for public investigation and possible legal action. The Staff Director of our merged organization had violated the terms of a $28,000 grant given us by the New York State Council on the Arts. The Attorney General must have felt he could build a case based on that indiscretion.

A young and enthusiastic Deputy Attorney General, who wanted me to know he "sat in Eliot Spitzer's chair in Albany" when that was a portentous place to sit, spearheaded the investigation. He searched vigorously to prove our Board had committed an illegal act. When belatedly I realized the misuse of the money and fired the Director, it was too late. Our records were subpoenaed.

I spent a "summer from hell" gathering the information demanded and then a grueling five-hour interrogation by the young Deputy Attorney General. The five hours ended abruptly when finally I was asked, "So what did you do?"

"I fired the guy!"

Neither arts organization exists any longer, and perhaps I'm somewhat wiser. There were useful things I could, but didn't, do. At its best, I loved working in and around the arts and artists for many years. My involvement with the League of Arts grew out of cooperative work we had done with the fine arts departments of several colleges.

After formally retiring from Hudson-Mohawk Association in 1986 I helped set up a not-for-profit organization to promote Albany's public Washington Park. I was the first President as the "Washington Park Conservancy" got underway; it's still active many years later. We developed a sizeable mailing list, a publication and regular meetings of friends and neighbors, and oversaw several useful improvements to the Park.

I was Chairman of the Board of our Unitarian Society in Schenectady for the usual term of two years and, with Sylvie, worked for many years on programs for Sunday morning services, including several dramatic programs I wrote and others, and the two of us, performed.

And here I am, with my own little book. I hope you've found it interesting.

Made in the USA
Charleston, SC
14 August 2014